The Noble Gentleman by Francis Beaumont & John Fletcher

The English dramatists Francis Beaumont and John Fletcher, collaborated in their writing during the reign of James I of England (James VI of Scotland, 1567–1625; in England he reigned from 1603).

Beaumont & Fletcher began to collaborate as writers soon after they met. After notable failures of their solo works their first joint effort, Philaster, was a success and tragicomedy was the genre they explored and built upon. There would be many further successes to follow.

There is an account that at the time the two men shared everything. They lived together in a house on the Bankside in Southwark, "they also lived together in Bankside, sharing clothes and having one wench in the house between them." Or as another account puts it "sharing everything in the closest intimacy."

Whatever the truth of this they were now recognised as perhaps the best writing team of their generation, so much so, that their joint names was applied to all the works in which either, or both, had a pen including those with Philip Massinger, James Shirley and Nathan Field.

The first Beaumont and Fletcher folio of 1647 contained 35 plays; 53 plays were included in the second folio in 1679. Other works bring the total plays in the canon to about 55. However there appears here to have been some duplicity on the account of the publishers who seemed to attribute so many to the team. It is now thought that the work between solely by Beaumont and Fletcher amounts to approximately 15 plays, though of course further works by them were re-worked by others and the originals lost.

After Beaumont's early death in 1616 Fletcher continued to write and, at his height was, by many standards, the equal of Shakespeare in popularity until his own death in 1625.

Index of Contents

DRAMATIS PERSONAE
SCENE: France.
PROLOGUE
ACTUS PRIMUS
SCÆNA PRIMA
ACTUS SECUNDUS
SCÆNA PRIMA
ACTUS TERTIUS
SCÆNA PRIMA
ACTUS QUARTUS
SCÆNA PRIMA
ACTUS QUINTUS
SCÆNA PRIMA
EPILOGUE
FRANCIS BEAUMONT – A SHORT BIOGRAPHY
JOHN FLETCHER – A SHORT BIOGRAPHY
FRANCIS BEAUMONT & JOHN FLETCHER – A CONCISE BIBLIOGRAPHY

MEN
Monsieur Marine, the Noble Gentleman but none of the wisest.
Jaques, an old servant to Marine's family.
Clerimont, a Gull, Cosin to Monsieur Marine.
A Gentleman, Servant to Marine's wife.
Longovile   } two Courtiers that plot
Beaufort   } to abuse Marine.
Shattillion, a Lord, mad for Love.
Doctor.
Page.
Gentlemen.
Servants.
Duke.
WOMEN
Marine's Wife, a witty wanton.
Clerimont's Wife, a simple countrey Gentlewoman.
Shattillion's Mistriss, a virtuous Virgin.
Maria, Servant to Marine's wife.
Duchess

SCENE: France.

PROLOGUE

Wit is become an Antick, and puts on
As many shapes of variation,
To court the times applause, as the times dare,
Change several fashions, nothing is thought rare
Which is not new, and follow'd, yet we know
That what was worn some twenty years agoe,
Comes into grace again, and we pursue
That custom, by presenting to your view
A Play in fashion then, not doubting now
But 'twill appear the same, if you allow
Worth to their noble memory, whose name,
Beyond all power of death, live in their fame.

ACTUS PRIMUS

SCÆNA PRIMA

Enter **GENTLEMAN** and **JAQUES**.

GENTLEMAN
What happiness waits on the life at Court,
What dear content, greatness, delight and ease!
What ever-springing hopes, what tides of honor!
That raise their fortunes to the height of wishes!
What can be more in man, what more in nature,
Than to be great and fear'd? A Courtier,
A noble Courtier, 'Tis a name that draws
Wonder and duty from all eyes and knees.

JAQUES
And so your Worships Land within the Walls,
Where you shall have it all inclos'd, and sure.

GENTLEMAN
Peace knave; dull creature, bred of sweat and smoke,
These mysteries are far above thy faith:
But thou shalt see—

JAQUES
And then I shall believe;
Your fair revenues, turn'd into fair suits;
I shall believe your Tenant's bruis'd and rent
Under the weight of Coaches, all your state
Drawn through the streets in triumph, suits for places
Plied with a Mine of Gold, and being got
Fed with a great stream. I shall believe all this.

GENTLEMAN
You shall believe, and know me glorious.
Cosin, good day and health.

[Enter **COSIN**.

COSIN
The same to you, Sir,
And more, without my wishes, could you know
What calm content dwels in a private house:
Yet look into your self, retire: this place
Of promises, and protestations, fits
Minds only bent to ruin, you should know this,
You have their language perfect, you have tutors
I do not doubt, sufficient: but beware.

GENTLEMAN
You are merry Cosin:

COSIN

Yet your patience,
You shall learn that too, but not like it self,
Where it is held a virtue; tell me Sir,
Have you cast up your State, rated your Land,
And find it able to endure the change
Of time and fashion? is it always harvest?
Always vintage? have you Ships at Sea,
To bring you Gold and Stone from rich Peru,
Monthly returning Treasure? doth the King
Open his large Exchequer to your hands
And bid ye be a great man? can your wife
Coin off her beauty? or the week allow
Suits to each day? and know no ebb in honor?
If these be possible, and can hold out,
Then be a Courtier still, and still be wasting.

GENTLEMAN

Cosin, pray give me leave:

COSIN

I have done.

GENTLEMAN

I could requite your gall, and in a strain
As bitter, and as full of Rubarb, preach
Against your Countrey life, but 'tis below me
And only subject to my pitty, know
The eminent Court, to them that can be wise,
And fasten on her blessings, is a Sun
That draws men up from course and earthly Being,
I mean these men of merit that have power
And reason to make good her benefits,
Learns them a manly boldness, gives their tongues
Sweetness of Language, makes them apt to please;
Files of all rudeness, and uncivil haviour,
Shews them as neat in carriage, as in cloaths;
Cosin, have you ever seen the Court?

COSIN

No Sir,
Nor am I yet in travel with that longing.

GENTLEMAN

Oh the state and greatness of that place
Where men are found
Only to give the first creation glory!

Those are the models of the antient world
Left like the Roman Statues to stir up
Our following hopes, the place it self puts on
The brow of Majesty, and flings her lustre
Like the air newly light'ned; Form, and Order,
Are only there themselves, unforc'd, and sound,
As they were first created to this place.

COSIN
You nobly came, but will goe from thence base.

GENTLEMAN
'Twas very pretty, and a good conceit;
You have a wit good Cosin, I do joy in't,
Keep it for Court: but to my self again,
When I have view'd these pieces, turn'd these eyes,
And with some taste of superstition,
Look'd on the wealth of Nature, the fair dames,
Beauties, that light the Court, and make it shew
Like a fair heaven, in a frosty night:
And 'mongst these mine, not poorest, 'tis for tongues
Of blessed Poets, such as Orpheus was,
To give their worth and praises; Oh dear Cosin:
You have a wife, and fair, bring her hither,
Let her not live to be the Mistriss of a Farmers heir
And be confin'd ever to a searge,
Far courser than my horse-cloth.
Let her have Velvets, Tiffinies, Jewels, Pearls,
A Coach, an Usher, and her two Lacquies,
And I will send my wife to give her rules,
And read the rudiments of Court to her.

COSIN
Sir, I had rather send her to Virginia
To help to propagate the English Nation.

[Enter **SERVANT**.

GENTLEMAN
Sirrah, how slept your Mistriss, and what visitants
Are to pay service?

SERVANT
As I came out,
Two Counts were newly ent'red.

GENTLEMAN
This is greatness,

But few such servants wait a Countrey beauty.

COSIN
They are the more to thank their modesty,
God keep my Wife, and all my Issue Female
From such uprisings.

[Enter a **DOCTOR**.

GENTLEMAN
What? my learned Doctor?
You will be welcome, give her health and youth
And I will give you gold.

[Exit **DOCTOR**.

Cosin, how savors this? is it not sweet
And very great, tasts it not of Nobleness?

COSIN
Faith Sir, my pallat is too dull and lazie
I cannot taste it, 'tis not for my relish,
But be so still.
Since your own misery must first reclaim ye,
To which I leave you, Sir,
If you will, yet be happy, leave the humor
And base subjection to your Wife, be wise,
And let her know with speed, you are her Husband,
I shall be glad to hear it.
My horse is sent for.

[Exit.

GENTLEMAN
Even such another countrey thing as this
Was I, such a piece of dirt, so heavy,
So provident to heap up ignorance,
And be an ass: such musty cloaths wore I,
So old and thred-bare, I do yet remember
Divers young Gallants lighting at my Gate,
To see my honoured Wife, have offered pence,
And bid me walk their horses, such a slave
Was I in shew then: but my eyes are open'd.

[Enter Gentleman **WIFE**.

Many sweet morrows to my worthy Wife.

WIFE
'Tis well, and aptly given, as much for you,
But to my present business, which is money—

GENTLEMAN
Lady, I have none left.

WIFE
I hope you dare not say so, nor imagine so base and low,
A thought: I have none left?
Are these words fitting for a man of worth,
And one of your full credit? Do you know
The place you live in? me? and what I labour
For, you? and your advancement?

GENTLEMAN
Yes my dearest.

WIFE
And do you pop me off with this slight answer,
In troth I have none left? in troth you must have;
Nay stare not, 'tis most true, send speedily
To all that love you, let your people flye
Like thunder, through the City,
And not return under five thousand Crowns.
Try all, take all, let not a wealthy Merchant be untempted
Or any one that hath the name of Money,
Take up at any Use, give Band, or Land,
Or mighty Statutes, able by their strength,
To tye up Sampson, were he now alive,
There must be money gotten; for be perswaded,
If we fall now, or be but seen to shrink,
Under our fair beginnings, 'tis our ruin,
And then good night to all, (but our disgrace)
Farewel the hope of coming happiness,
And all the aims we levied at so long.
Are ye not mov'd at this? no sense of want,
Towards your self yet breeding? be old,
And common; jaded to the eyes
Of Grooms, and Pages, Chamber-maids, and Guarders,
And when you have done, put your poor house in order
And hang your self, for such must be the end
Of him that willingly forsakes his hopes
And hath a joy to tumble to his ruin.
All that I say is certain, if ye fail
Do not impute me with it, I am clear.

GENTLEMAN

Now heaven forbid I should do wrong to you
My dearest Wife, and Madam; yet give leave
To your poor creature to unfold himself.
You know my debts are many more than means,
My bands not taken in, my friends at home
Drawn dry with these expences, my poor Tenants
More full of want than we, then what new course
Can I beget, to raise those crowns by? speak,
And I shall execute.

WIFE
Pray tell me true,
Have you not Land in the Countrey?

GENTLEMAN
Pardon me, I had forgot it.

WIFE
Sir, you must remember it,
There is no remedy, this Land must be,
In Paris e'r to morrow night.

GENTLEMAN
It shall, let me consider, some 300 acres
Will serve the turn.

WIFE
'Twill furnish at all points,
Now you speak like your self, and know like him,
That means to be a man, suspect no less
For the return will give ye five for one,
You shall be great to morrow, I have said it.
Farewel, and see this business be a-foot,
With expedition.

[Exit **WIFE**.

GENTLEMAN
Health, all joy, and honor
Wait on my lovely Wife.
What? Jaques, Jaques.

[Enter **JAQUES**.

JAQUES
Sir, did you call?

GENTLEMAN

I did so, hie thee Jaques.
Down to the Bank, and there to some good Merchant
(Conceive me well, good Jaques, and be private)
Offer 300 acres of my Land:
Say it is choice and fertile, ask upon it
Five thousand Crowns, this is the business
I must employ thee in, be wise and speedy.

JAQUES
Sir, do not do this.

GENTLEMAN
Knave, I must have money.

JAQUES
If you have money thus, your knave must tell ye
You will not have a foot of Land left, be more wary,
And more friend to your self, this honest Land
Your Worship has discarded, has been true,
And done you loyal service.

GENTLEMAN
Gentle Jaques,
You have a merry wit, employ it well
About the business you have now in hand.
When ye come back, enquire me in the Presence,
If not in the Tennis-Court, or at my house.

[Exit.

JAQUES
If this vain hold, I know where to enquire ye.
Five thousand Crowns! this, with good husbandry,
May hold a month out, then 5000 more,
And more Land a bleeding for't, as many more,
And more Land laid aside. God and St. Dennis
Keep honest minded young men batchelors.
'Tis strange, my Master should be yet so young
A puppy, that he cannot see his fall
And got so near the Sun. I'll to his Cosin.
And once more tell him on't, if he fail,
Then to my Mortgage, next unto my sale.

[Exit.

[Enter **LONGOVILE, BEWFORD** and the **SERVANT**.

SERVANT

Gentlemen, hold on discourse a while,
I shall return with knowledge how and where
We shall have best access unto my Mistriss
To tender your devotions.

[Exit.

LONGOVILE
Be it so:
Now to our first discourse.

BEWFORD
I prethee peace;
Thou canst not be so bad, or make me know
Such things are living, do not give thy self
So common and so idle, so open vile,
So great a wronger of thy worth, so low,
I cannot, nor I must not credit thee.

LONGOVILE
Now by this light I am a whoremaster,
An open, and an excellent whormaster,
And take a special glory that I am so:
I thank my Stars I am a whoremaster,
And such a one as dare be known and seen,
And pointed at to be a noble wencher.

BEWFORD
Do not let all ears hear this, hark ye Sir,
I am my self a whoremaster, I am
Believe it Sir (in private be it spoken)
I love a whore directly, most men are wenchers,
And have profest the Science, few men
That look upon ye now, but whoremasters,
Or have a full desire to be so.

LONGOVILE
This is noble.

BEWFORD
It is without all question, being private,
And held as needful as intelligence,
But being once discover'd, blown abroad,
And known to common senses, 'tis no more
Than geometrical rules in Carpenters,
That only know some measure of an Art,
But are not grounded: be no more deceived,
I have a conscience to reclaim you, Sir.

Mistake me not: I do not bid you leave your whore
Or less to love her; forbid it,
I should be such a villain to my friend,
Or so unnatural: 'twas never harbor'd here,
Learn to be secret first, then strike your Deer.

LONGOVILE
Your fair instructions, Monsieur, I shall learn.

BEWFORD
And you shall have them; I desire your care.

LONGOVILE
They are your servants.

BEWFORD
You must not love.

LONGOVILE
How Sir?

BEWFORD
I mean a Lady, there's danger.
She hath an Usher and a Waiting Gentlewoman,
A Page, a Coach-man, these are fee'd and fee'd
And yet for all that will be prating.

LONGOVILE
So.

BEWFORD
You understand me Sir, they will discover't,
And there is a loss of credit, Table-talk
Will be the end of this, or worse, than that;
Will this be worthy of a Gentleman?

LONGOVILE
Proceed good Sir.

BEWFORD
Next leave your City Dame;
The best of that Tribe, are most meerly coy,
Or most extreamly foolish, both which vices
Are no great stirrers up, unless in Husbands
That owe this Cattle, fearing her that's coy
To be but seeming, her that's fool too forward.

LONGOVILE

This is the rarest fellow, and the soundest,
I mean in knowledge, that e'r wore a Codpiece,
H'as found out that will pass all Italy,
All France and England; to their shames I speak,
And to the griefs of all their Gentlemen,
The noble Theory of Luxury.

BEWFORD
Your patience,
And I will lay before your eyes a course
That I my self found out, 'tis excellent,
Easie, and full of freedome.

LONGOVILE
O good Sir,
You rack me till I know it.

BEWFORD
This it is,
When your desire is up, your blood well heated
And apt for sweet encounter, chuse the night,
And with the night your Wench, the streets have store,
There seize upon her, get her to your chamber,
Give her a cardecew, 'tis royal payment;
When ye are dull, dismiss her, no man knows,
Nor she her self, who hath encountred her.

LONGOVILE
O but their faces.

BEWFORD
Nere talke of faces:
The night allows her equal with a Dutchess,
Imagination doth all think her fair,
And great, clapt in Velvet, she is so,
Sir, I have tryed those, and do find it certain
It never failes me, 'tis but twelve nights since
My last experience.

LONGOVILE
O my meiching Varlet, I'll fit ye as I live.
'Tis excellent, I'll be your Scholar Sir.

[Enter **LADY** and **SERVANT**.

WIFE
You are fairly welcome both: troth Gentlemen
You have been strangers, I could chide you for't,

And taxe ye with unkindness, What's the news?
The Town was never empty of some novelty;
Servant, What's your intelligence?

SERVANT
Faith nothing.
I have not heard of any worth relating.

BEWFORD
Nor I sweet Lady.

LONGOVILE
Then give me attention,
Monsieur Shattillion's mad.

WIFE
Mad?

LONGOVILE
Mad as May-butter,
And which is more, mad for a Wench.

LADY
'Tis strange, and full of pity.

LONGOVILE
All that comes near him
He thinks are come of purpose to betray him,
Being full of strange conceit: the wench he loved
Stood very near the Crown.

LADY
Alass good Monsieur;
A' was a proper man, and fair demean'd,
A Person worthy of a better temper.

LONGOVILE
He is strong opinion'd that the Wench he lov'd
Remains close prisoner by the Kings command:
Fearing her title, when the poor grieved Gentlewoman
Follows him much lamenting, and much loving
In hope to make him well, he knows her not,
Nor any else that comes to visit him.

LADY
Let's walk in Gentlemen, and there discourse
His further miseries, you shall stay dinner,
In truth you must obey.

OMNES
We are your servants.

[Exeunt.

[Enter **COSIN**.

COSIN
There's no good to be done, no cure to be wrought
Upon my desperate Kinsman: I'll to horse
And leave him to the fools whip, misery.
I shall recover twenty miles this night,
My horse stands ready, I'll away with speed.

[Enter **SHATTILLION**.

SHATTILLION
Sir, may I crave your name?

COSIN
Yes Sir you may:
My name is Cleremont.

SHATTILLION
'Tis well, your faction?
What party knit you with?

COSIN
I know no parties,
Nor no Factions, Sir.

SHATTILLION
Then weare this Cross of white:
And where you see the like they are my friends,
Observe them well, the time is dangerous.

COSIN
Sir keep your cross, I'll weare none, sure this fellow
Is much beside himself, grown mad.

SHATTILLION
A word Sir;
You can pick nothing out of this, this cross
Is nothing but a cross, a very cross,
Plain, without spell, or witchcraft, search it,
You may suspect, and well, there's poyson in't,
Powder, or wild-fire, but 'tis nothing so.

COSIN

I do believe you, Sir, 'tis a plain cross.

SHATTILLION

Then do your worst, I care not, tell the King,
Let him know all this, as I am sure he shall;
When you have spit your venome, then will I
Stand up a faithful, and a loyal Subject,
And so God save His Grace, this is no Treason.

COSIN

He is March mad, farewell Monsieur.

[Exit **COSIN**.

SHATTILLION

Farewel;
I shall be here attending, 'tis my life
They aime at, there's no way to save it, well
Let 'em spread all their nets: they shall not draw me
Into any open Treason, I can see,
And can beware, I have my wits about me,
I thank heaven for't.

[Enter **LOVE**.

LOVE

There he goes,
That was the fairest hope the French Court bred,
The worthiest and the sweetest temper'd spirit,
The truest, and the valiantest, the best of judgment,
Till most unhappy I: sever'd those virtues,
And turn'd his wit wild with a coy denial,
Which heaven forgive me, and be pleas'd, O heaven
To give again his senses: that my love
May strike off all my follies.

SHATTILLION

Lady.

LOVE

I Sir.

SHATTILLION

Your will with me sweet Lady.

LOVE

Sir, I come.

SHATTILLION
From the dread sovereign King, I know it Lady,
He is a gracious Prince, long may he live,
Pertain you to his chamber?

LOVE
No indeed Sir,
That place is not for women, Do you know me?

SHATTILLION
Yes, I do know you.

LOVE
What's my name? pray you speak.

SHATTILLION
That's all one, I do know you and your business,
You are discover'd Lady, I am wary,
It stands upon my life; pray excuse me,
The best man of this Kingdom sent you hither,
To dive into me, have I toucht you? ha?

LOVE
You are deceiv'd Sir, I come from your love,
That sends you fair commends, and many kisses.

SHATTILLION
Alass, poor soul, How does she? Is she living?
Keeps she her bed still?

LOVE
Still Sir, She is living,
And well, and shall do so.

SHATTILLION
Are ye in counsel?

LOVE
No Sir, nor any of my sex.

SHATTILLION
Why so,
If you had been in counsel, you would know,
Her time to be but slender; she must die.

LOVE

I do believe it, Sir.

SHATTILLION
And suddenly,
She stands too near a fortune.

LOVE
Sir?

SHATTILLION
'Tis so,
There is no jesting with a Princes Title,
Would we had both been born of common parents,
And liv'd a private and retir'd life,
In homely cottage, we had then enjoyed,
Our loves, and our embraces, these are things,
That cannot tend to Treason—

LOVE
I am wretched.

SHATTILLION
O I pray as often for the King as any,
And with as true a heart, for's continuance,
And do moreover pray his heirs may live;
And their fair issues, then as I am bound
For all the states and commons: if these prayers
Be any wayes ambitious, I submit,
And lay my head down, let 'em take it off;
You may informe against me, but withall
Remember my obedience to the Crown,
And service to the State.

LOVE
Good Sir, I love ye.

SHATTILLION
Then love the gracious King, and say with me.

LOVE
Heaven save his Grace.

SHATTILLION
This is strange—
A woman should be sent to undermine me,
And buz love into me to try my spirit;
Offer me kisses, and enticing follies,
To make me open, and betray my self;

It was a subtile and a dangerous plot,
And very soundly followed, farewel Lady,
Let me have equal hearing, and relate
I am an honest Man. Heaven save the King.

[Exit.

LOVE
I'll never leave him, till, by art or prayer,
I have restor'd his senses, If I make
Him perfect Man again, he's mine, till when,
I here abjure all loves of other men.

[Exit.

[Enter **COSIN**, and **JAQUES**.

JAQUES
Nay, good Sir be perswaded, go but back,
And tell him hee's undone, say nothing else;
And you shall see how things will work upon't.

COSIN
Not so good Jaques, I am held an asse,
A Countrey Fool, good to converse with dirt,
And eate course bread, weare the worst Wooll,
Know nothing but the high-way to Paris,
And wouldst thou have me bring these stains,
And imperfections to the rising view
Of the right worshipful thy worthy Master?
They must be bright, and shine, their cloaths
Soft Velvet, and the Tyrian Purple
Like the Arabian gums, hung like the Sun,
Their golden beames on all sides;
Such as these may come and know
Thy Master, I am base, and dare not speak unto him,
Hee's above me.

JAQUES
If ever you did love him, or his state,
His name, his issue, or your self, go back:
'Twill be an honest and a noble part
Worthy a Kinsman; save 300 Acres
From present execution; they have had sentence,
And cannot be repriev'd, be merciful.

COSIN
Have I not urg'd already all the reasons,

I had to draw him from his will? his ruin?
But all in vain, no counsel will prevail;
H'as fixt himself, there's no removing, Jaques,
'Twill prove but breath and labor spent in vain,
I'll to my horse, farewell.

JAQUES
For Gods sake, Sir,
As ever you have hope of joy, turn back;
I'll be your slave for ever, do but go,
And I will lay such fair directions to you
That if he be not doting on his fall,
He shall recover sight, and see his danger,
And ye shall tell him of his Wives abuses,
I fear, too foul against him; how she plots,
With our young Mounsiers, to milk-dry her husband,
And lay it on their backs; the next her pride;
Then what his debts are, and how infinite
The curses of his Tenants, this will work
I'll pawn my life and head, he cries away,
I'll to my house in the Countrey.

COSIN
Come, I'll go, and once more try him,
If he yield not, so,
The next that tryes him shall be want and woe.

[Exeunt.

ACTUS SECUNDUS

SCÆNA PRIMA

[Enter **GENTLEMAN, SOLUS**.

GENTLEMAN
Jaques.

JAQUES [within]
Sir.

GENTLEMAN
Rise Jaques 'tis grown day,
The Country life is best, where quietly,
Free from the clamor of the troubled Court,
We may enjoy our own green shadowed walks,

And keep a moderate diet without art.
Why did I leave my house, and bring my Wife,
To know the manner of this subtile place?
I would, when first the lust to fame and honor,
Possest me, I had met with any evil,
But that; had I been tied to stay at home,
And earn the bread for the whole family,
With my own hand, happy had I been.

[Enter **JAQUES**.

JAQUES
Sir, this is from your wonted course at home,
When did ye there keep such inordinate hours?
Goe to bed late? start thrice? and call on me?
Would you were from this place; our Countrey sleeps,
Although they were but of that moderate length
That might maintain us in our daily work,
Yet were they sound and sweet.

GENTLEMAN
I Jaques, there we dreamt not of our Wives, we lay together;
And needed not; now at length my Cousin's words,
So truly meant, mixt with thy timely prayers
So often urged, to keep me at my home,
Condemn me quite.

JAQUES
'Twas not your fathers course:
He liv'd and dy'd in Orleance, where he had
His Vines as fruitful as experience
(Which is the art of Husbandry) could make;
He had his presses for 'em, and his wines
Were held the best, and out-sold other Mens,
His corn and cattel serv'd the neighbor Towns
With plentiful provision, yet his thrift
Could miss one Beast amongst the heard;
He rul'd more where he liv'd, than ever you will here.

GENTLEMAN
'Tis true, why should my Wife then, 'gainst my good,
Perswade me to continue in this course?

JAQUES
Why did you bring her hither at the first,
Before you warm'd her blood with new delights?
Our Countrey sports could have contented her;
When you first married her a puppet-play

Pleas'd her as well as now the tilting doth.
She thought her self brave in a bugle chain,
Where Orient pearl will scarce content her now.

GENTLEMAN
Sure Jaques, she sees something for my good
More than I do; she oft will talk to me
Of Offices, and that she shortly hopes,
By her acquaintance with the friends she hath,
To get a place shall many times outweigh
Our great expences, and if this be so—

JAQUES
Think better of her words, she doth deceive you,
And only for her vain and sensual ends
Perswade ye thus. Let me be set to dwell
For ever naked in the barest soil,
So you will dwell from hence.

GENTLEMAN
I see my folly,
Pack up my stuffe, I will away this morne.
Haste—haste.

JAQUES
I, now I see your Father's honors
Trebling upon you, and the many prayers
The Countrey spent for him, which almost now
Begun to turn to curses, turning back,
And falling like a timely shower
Upon ye.

GENTLEMAN
Goe, call up my Wife.

JAQUES
But shall she not prevail,
And sway you, as she oft hath done before?

GENTLEMAN
I will not hear her, but raile on her,
Till I be ten miles off.

JAQUES
If you be forty,
'Twill not be worse Sir:

GENTLEMAN

Call her up.

JAQUES
I will Sir.

[Exit.

GENTLEMAN
Why what an Ass was I that such a thing
As a Wife is could rule me!
Know not I that woman was created for the man,
That her desires, nay all her thoughts should be
As his are? is my sense restor'd at length?
Now she shall know, that which she should desire,
She hath a husband that can govern her,

[Enter **WIFE**.

If her desires leads me against my will;
Are you come?

WIFE
What sad unwonted course
Makes you raise me so soon, that went to bed
So late last-night.

GENTLEMAN
O you shall goe to bed sooner hereafter,
And be rais'd again at thrifty hours:
In Summer time wee'l walk
An hour after our Supper, and to bed,
In Winter you shall have a set at Cards,
And set your Maids to work.

WIFE
What do you mean?

GENTLEMAN
I will no more of your new tricks, your honors,
Your Offices, and all your large preferments,
Which still you beat into my ears, hang o'er me,
I'll leave behind for others, the great sway
Which I shall bear at Court: my living here
With countenance of your honoured friends,
I'll be content to lose: for you speak this
Only that you may still continue here
In wanton ease: and draw me to consume,
In cloaths and other things idle for shew,

That which my Father got with honest thrift.

WIFE
Why, who hath been with you Sir,
That you talk thus out of Frame.

GENTLEMAN
You make a fool of me:
You provide one to bid me forth to supper,
And make me promise; then must some one or other
Invite you forth, if you have born your self
Loosely to any Gentleman in my sight
At home, you ask me how I like the carriage,
Whether it were not rarely for my good,
And open'd not a way to my preferment?
Come, I perceive all: talk not, we'll away.

WIFE
Why Sir, you'll stay till the next triumph
Day be past?

GENTLEMAN
I, you have kept me here triumphing
This seven years, and I have ridden through the streets,
And bought embroyder'd hose and foot-cloths too,
To shew a subjects zeal, I rode before
In this most gorgeous habit, and saluted
All the acquaintance I could espie
From any window, these are wayes ye told me
To raise me; I see all: make you ready straight,
And in that Gown which you came first to Town in,
Your safe-guard, cloak, and your hood sutable:
Thus on a double gelding shall you amble,
And my man Jaques shall be set before you.

WIFE
But will you goe?

GENTLEMAN
I will.

WIFE
And shall I too?

GENTLEMAN
And you shall too.

WIFE

But shall I by this light?

GENTLEMAN
Why by this light you shall.

WIFE
Then by this light
You have no care of your Estate, and mine.
Have we been seven years venturing in a Ship,
And now upon return, with a fair wind,
And a calm Sea, full fraught with our own wishes,
Laden with wealth and honor to the brim,
And shall we flye away and not receive it?
Have we been tilling, sowing, labouring,
With pain and charge a long and tedious winter,
And when we see the corn above the ground,
Youthful as is the Morn and the full eare,
That promises to stuffe our spacious garners,
Shall we then let it rot, and never reap it?

GENTLEMAN
Wife talke no more, your Rhetorick comes too late,
I am inflixible; and how dare you
Adventure to direct my course of life?
Was not the husband made to rule the Wife?

WIFE
'Tis true: but where the man doth miss his way,
It is the Womans part to set him right;
So Fathers have a power to guide their Sons
In all their courses, yet you oft have seen
Poor little children, that have both their eyes,
Lead their blind Fathers.

GENTLEMAN
She has a plaguy wit,
I say you'r but a little piece of man.

WIFE
But such a piece, as being tane away,
Man cannot last: the fairest and tallest ship,
That ever sail'd, is by a little piece of the same
Wood, steer'd right, and turn'd about.

GENTLEMAN
'Tis true she sayes, her answers stand with reason.

WIFE

But Sir, your Cozin put this in your head,
Who is an enemy to your preferment,
Because I should not take place of his wife;
Come, by this kiss, thou shalt not go sweet heart.

GENTLEMAN
Come, by this kiss I will go Sweet-heart,
On with your riding stuffe: I know your tricks,
And if preferment fall ere you be ready,
'Tis welcome, else adieu the City life.

WIFE
Well, Sir, I will obey.

GENTLEMAN
About it then.

WIFE
To please your humor I would dress my self,
In the most loathsome habit you could name,
Or travel any whether o're the World,
If you command me, it shall ne'r be said,
The frailty of a woman, whose weak mind,
Is often set on loose delights, and shews,
Hath drawn her husband to consume his state,
In the vain hope of that which never fell.

GENTLEMAN
About it then, women are pleasant creatures,
When once a man begins to know himself.

WIFE
But hark you Sir, because I will be sure,
You shall have no excuse, no word to say
In your defence hereafter; when you see
What honors were prepar'd for you and me,
Which you thus willingly have thrown away,
I tell you I did look for present honor,
This morning for you, which I know had come:
But if they do not come ere I am ready
(Which I will be the sooner least they should)
When I am once set in a countrey life,
Not all the power of earth shall alter me,
Not all your prayers or threats shall make me speak
The least words to my honorable friends,
To do you any grace.

GENTLEMAN

I will not wish it.

WIFE
And never more hope to be honorable.

GENTLEMAN
My hopes are lower.

WIFE
As I live you shall not,
You shall be so far from the name of noble
That you shall never see a Lord again;
You shall not see a Maske, or Barriers,
Or Tilting, or a solemn Christning,
Or a great Marriage, or new Fire-works,
Or any bravery; but you shall live
At home, bespotted with your own lov'd durt,
In scurvy cloaths, as you were wont to doe,
And to content you, I will live so too.

GENTLEMAN
Tis all I wish, make haste, the day draws on,
It shall be my care to see your Stuffe packt up.

WIFE
It shall be my care to gull you: you shall stay.

[Exit **GENTLEMAN**.

And more than so, intreat me humbly too,
You shall have honors presently; Maria.

[Enter **MARIA**.

MARIA
Madam.

WIFE
Bring hither, pen, ink, and paper.

MARIA
'Tis here.

WIFE
Your Master will not stay,
Unless preferment come within an hour.

MARIA

Let him command one of the City gates,
In time of mutiny, or you may provide him,
To be one of the counsel for invading,
Some savage Countrey to plant Christian faith.

WIFE
No, no, I have it for him, call my page;
Now, my dear husband, there it is will fit you.

[Exit **MARIA**.

And when the world shall see what I have done,
Let it not move the spleen of any Wife,
To make an Ass of her beloved husband,
Without good ground, but if they will be drawn
To any reason by you, do not gull them;
But if they grow conceited of themselves,
And be fine Gentlemen, have no mercy,
Publish them to the World, 'twill do them good
When they shall see their follies understood,
Go bear these Letters to my servant,
And bid him make haste, I will dress my self,
In all the Journey-Cloaths I us'd before,
Not to ride, but to make the Laughter more.

[Exit.

[Enter **GENTLEMAN** and **JAQUES**.

GENTLEMAN
Is all packt up?

JAQUES
All, all Sir, there is no tumbler
Runs through his hoop with more dexterity,
Then I about this business: 'Tis a day,
That I have long long'd to see.

GENTLEMAN
Come, Where's my Spurs?

JAQUES
Here, Sir, and now 'tis come.

GENTLEMAN
I, Jaques, now,
I thank my fates, I can command my Wife.

JAQUES
I am glad to see it, Sir.

GENTLEMAN
I do not love always,
To be made a puppie, Jaques.

JAQUES
But, yet me thinks your Worship does not look,
Right like a Countrey Gentleman.

GENTLEMAN
I will, give me my t'other hat.

JAQUES
Here.

GENTLEMAN
So, my Jerkin.

JAQUES
Yes, Sir.

GENTLEMAN
On with it Jaques, thou and I
Will live so finely in the Countrey, Jaques,
And have such pleasant walks into the Woods
A mornings, and then bring home riding-rods,
And walking staves—

JAQUES
And I will bear them, Sir,
And Skurdge-sticks for the children.

GENTLEMAN
So thou shalt,
And thou shalt do all, over-see my Work-folkes,
And at the weeks end pay them all their wages.

JAQUES
I will, Sir, so your Worship give me Money.

GENTLEMAN
Thou shalt receive all too: give me my Drawers.

JAQUES
They are ready, Sir.

GENTLEMAN
And I will make thy Mistriss,
My wife, look to her landrie, and her dairy,
That we may have our linnen clean on Sundayes.

JAQUES
And Holy-dayes.

GENTLEMAN
I, and ere we walk about the Grounds
Provide our break-fast,
Or she shall smoke, I'll have her a good huswife;
She shall not make a voyage to her Sisters,
But she shall live at home,
And feed her pullen fat, and see her Maides
In bed before her, and lock all the doors.

JAQUES
Why that will be a life for Kings and Queens.

GENTLEMAN
Give me my Scarfe with the great Button quickly.

JAQUES
'Tis done, Sir.

GENTLEMAN
Now my Mittens.

JAQUES
Here they are, Sir.

GENTLEMAN
'Tis well: now my great dagger.

JAQUES
There.

GENTLEMAN
Why so; thus it should be, now my riding rod.

JAQUES
There's nothing wanting, Sir.

GENTLEMAN
Another, man, to stick under my girdle.

JAQUES

There it is.

GENTLEMAN
All is well.

JAQUES
Why now methinks your Worship looks
Like to your self, a Man of means and credit,
So did your grave and famous Ancestors,
Ride up and down to Fairs, and cheapen cattel.

GENTLEMAN
Goe, hasten your Mistriss, Sirra.

JAQUES
It shall be done.

[Exit **JAQUES**.

[Enter **SERVANT** and **PAGE**.

SERVANT
Who's that? who's that Boy?

PAGE
I think it be my Master.

SERVANT
Who, he that walkes in gray, whisking his riding rod?

PAGE
Yes, Sir, 'tis he.

SERVANT
'Tis he indeed; he is prepar'd
For his new journey; when I wink upon you,
Run out and tell the Gentleman 'tis time—
Monsieur good day.

GENTLEMAN
Monsieur, your Mistriss is within, but yet not ready.

SERVANT
My business is with you, Sir; 'tis reported,
I know not whether by some enemy
Maliciously, that envies your great hopes,
And would be ready to sow discontents
Betwixt his Majesty, and you, or truely,

Which on my faith I would be sorry for,
That you intend to leave the Court in haste.

GENTLEMAN
Faith, Sir, within this half hour. Jaques?

Jaques within: Sir?

GENTLEMAN
Is my Wife ready?

JAQUES
Presently.

SERVANT
But Sir,
I needs must tell you, as I am your friend,
You should have ta'en your journey privater,
For 'tis already blaz'd about the Court.

GENTLEMAN
Why Sir, I hope it is no Treason, is it?

SERVANT
'Tis true, Sir, but 'tis grown the common talk,
There's no discovery else held, and in the presence
All the Nobility and Gentry,
Have nothing in their mouths but only this,
Monsieur Marine, that noble Gentleman,
Is now departing hence: every Mans face
Looks ghastly on his fellows; such a sadness
(Before this day) I ne'er beheld in Court,
Mens hearts begin to fail them when they hear it,
In expectation of the great event
That needs must follow it, pray Heaven it be good!

GENTLEMAN
Why, I had rather all their hearts should fail,
Than I stay here until my purse fail me.

SERVANT
But yet you are a Subject, and beware,
I charge you by the love I bear to you,
How you do venture rashly on a course,
To make your Sovereign jealous of your deeds,
For Princes jealousies, where they love most,
Are easily found, but they be hardly lost.

GENTLEMAN
Come, these are tricks, I smell 'em, I will goe.

SERVANT
Have I not still profest my self your friend?

GENTLEMAN
Yes, but you never shewd it to me yet.

SERVANT
But now I will, because I see you wise,
And give ye thus much light into a business,
That came to me but now, be resolute,
Stand stifly to it that you will depart,
And presently.

GENTLEMAN
Why so I mean to doe.

SERVANT
And by this light you may be what you will;
Will you be secret, Sir?

GENTLEMAN
Why? What's the matter?

SERVANT
The King does fear you.

GENTLEMAN
How?

SERVANT
And is now in Counsel;

GENTLEMAN
About me?

SERVANT
About you, and you be wise,
You'll find he's in Counsel about you:
His Counsellors have told him all the truth.

GENTLEMAN
What truth?

SERVANT
Why, that which now he knows too well.

GENTLEMAN
What is't?

SERVANT
That you have followed him seven years,
With a great train: and though he have not grac't you,
Yet you have div'd into the hearts of thousands,
With liberality and noble carriage;
And if you should depart home unprefer'd,
All discontented, and seditious spirits
Would flock to you, and thrust you into action:
With whose help, and your Tenants, who doth not know
(If you were so dispos'd:)
How great a part of this yet fertile peaceful Realm of France
You might make desolate? but when the King
Heard this—

GENTLEMAN
What said he?

SERVANT
Nothing, but shook,
As never Christian Prince did shake before.
And to be short, you may be what you will
But be not ambitious Sir, sit down
With moderate honors, least you make your self
More fear'd.

GENTLEMAN
I know, Sir, what I have to doe
In mine own business.

[Enter **LONGOVILE**.

LONGOVILE
Where's Monsieur Mount Marine?

SERVANT
Why there he stands, will you ought with him?

LONGOVILE
Yes: Good day Monsieur Marine.

GENTLEMAN
Good day to you.

LONGOVILE

His Majesty doth commend himself,
Most kindly to you Sir, and hath, by me,
Sent you this favor: kneel down, rise a Knight.

GENTLEMAN
I thank his Majesty.

LONGOVILE
And he doth further request you,
Not to leave the Court so soon,
For though your former merits have been slighted,
After this time there shall no Office fall;
Worthy your spirit, as he doth confess
There's none so great, but you shall surely have it.

SERVANT
Do you hear? if you yield yet you are an ass.

GENTLEMAN
I'll shew my service to his Majesty
In greater things than these, but for this small one
I must intreat his Highness to excuse me.

LONGOVILE
I'll bear your Knightly words unto the King,
And bring his Princely answer back again.

[Exit **LONGOVILE**.

SERVANT
Well said, be resolute a while, I know
There is a tide of honors coming on.
I warrant you.

[Enter **BEWFORD**.

BEWFORD
Where is this new made Knight?

GENTLEMAN
Here, Sir.

BEWFORD
Let me enfold you in my arms,
Then call you Lord, the King will have it so,
Who doth entreat your Lordship to remember
His Message sent to you by Longovile.

SERVANT
If ye be durty, and dare not mount aloft;
You may yield now, I know what I would do.

GENTLEMAN
Peace, I will fit him; tell his Majesty
I am a Subject, and I do confess
I serve a gracious Prince, that thus hath heapt
Honors on me without desert, but yet
As for the Message, business urgeth me,
I must be gone, and he must pardon me,
Were he ten thousand Kings and Emperors.

BEWFORD
I'll tell him so.

SERVANT
Why, this was like your self.

BEWFORD
As he hath wrought him, 'tis the finest fellow
That e're was Christmas Lord, he carries it
So truely to the life, as though he were
One of the plot to gull himself.

[Exit **BEWFORD**.

SERVANT
Why so, you sent the wisest and the shrewdest answer
Unto the King, I swear, my honored friend,
That ever any Subject sent his Liege.

GENTLEMAN
Nay now I know I have him on the hip,
I'll follow it.

[Enter **LONGOVILE**.

LONGOVILE
My honorable Lord,
Give me your noble hand right courteous Peer,
And from henceforth be a courtly Earl;
The King so wills, and Subjects must obey:
Only he doth desire you to consider
Of his request.

SERVANT
Why faith you'r well my Lord, yield to him.

GENTLEMAN
Yield? why 'twas my plot.

SERVANT
Nay, 'twas your Wives plot.

GENTLEMAN
To get preferment by it,
And thinks he now to pop me i'th' mouth
But with an Earldome? I'll be one step higher.

SERVANT
'Tis the finest Lord, I am afraid anon
He will stand upon't to share the Kingdom with him.

[Enter **BEWFORD**.

BEWFORD
Where's this Courtly Earl?
His Majesty commends his love unto you;
And will you but now grant to his request,
He bids you be a Duke, and chuse of whence.

SERVANT
Why if you yield not now, you are undone,
What can you wish to have more, but the Kingdom?

GENTLEMAN
So please his Majesty, I would be Duke of Burgundy,
Because I like the place.

BEWFORD
I know the King is pleas'd.

GENTLEMAN
Then will I stay and kiss his Highness hand.

BEWFORD
His Majesty will be a glad man when he hears it.

LONGOVILE
But how shall we keep this from the world's ear,
That some one tell him not, he is no Duke?

SERVANT
Wee'l think of that anon.
Why Gentlemen, Is this a gracious habit for a Duke?

Each gentle body set a finger to
To pluck the clouds of this his riding weeds
From off the orient Sun of his best cloaths;
I'll pluck one Boot and spur off.

LONGOVILE
I another.

BEWFORD
I'll pluck his Jerkin off.

SERVANT
Sit down my Lord;
Both his spurs off at once good Longovile,
And Bewford, take that Scarfe off, and that Hat,
Doth not become his largely sprouting fore-head.
Now set your gracious foot to this of mine,
One pluck will do it, so, off with the other.

LONGOVILE
Loe, thus your servant Longovile doth pluck
The trophy of your former gentry off.
Off with his Jerkin Bewford.

SERVANT
Didst thou never see
A nimble footed Taylor stand so in his stockings,
Whilst some friend help'd to pluck his Jerkin off,
To dance a Jigg?

[Enter **JAQUES**.

LONGOVILE
Here's his man Jaques come,
Booted and ready still.

JAQUES
My Mistriss stayes;
Why how now Sir? What do's your Worship mean,
To pluck your grave and thrifty habit off.

GENTLEMAN
My slippers, Jaques.

LONGOVILE
O thou mighty Duke,
Pardon this Man,
That thus hath trespassed in ignorance.

GENTLEMAN
I pardon him.

LONGOVILE
His Graces slippers, Jaques.

JAQUES
Why what's the matter?

LONGOVILE
Foot-man, he's a Duke:
The King hath rais'd him above all his Land.

JAQUES
I'll to his Cosin presently, and tell him so;
O what a dung-hill Countrey rogue was I.

[Exit **JAQUES**.

[Enter **WIFE**.

SERVANT
See, see, my Mistriss.

LONGOVILE
Let's observe their greeting.

WIFE
Unto your will, as every good Wife ought,
I have turn'd all my thoughts, and now am ready.

GENTLEMAN
O Wife, I am not worthy to kiss the least
Of all thy toes, much less thy Thumb,
Which yet I would be bold with; all thy counsel
Hath been to me Angelical, but mine to thee
Hath been most dirty, like my mind:
Dear Duchess I must stay.

WIFE
What are you mad, to make me
Dress, and undress, turn and wind me,
Because you find me plyant? said I not
The whole world should not alter me, if once
I were resolv'd? and now you call me Duchess:
Why what's the matter?

GENTLEMAN
Loe a Knight doth kneel.

WIFE
A Knight?

GENTLEMAN
A Lord.

WIFE
A Fool.

GENTLEMAN
I say doth kneel an Earl, a Duke.

LONGOVILE
In Drawers.

BEWFORD
Without shoes.

WIFE
Sure you are lunatick.

SERVANT
No, honoured Duchess,
If you dare but believe your servants truth,
I know he is a Duke.

LONGOVILE
God save his Grace.

WIFE
I ask your Graces pardon.

GENTLEMAN
Then I rise,
And here, in token that all strife shall end,
'Twixt thee and me, I let my drawers fall,
And to thy hands I do deliver them:
Which signifies, that in all acts and speeches,
From this time forth, my Wife shall wear the breeches.

SERVANT
An honorable composition.

[Exeunt **OMNES**.

Enter **COSIN**, and **JAQUES**.

COSIN
Shall I believe thee, Jaques?

JAQUES
Sir you may.

COSIN
Didst thou not dreame?

JAQUES
I did not.

COSIN
Nor imagine?

JAQUES
Neither of both: I saw him great and mighty,
I saw the Monsieurs bow, and heard them cry,
Good health and fortune to my Lord the Duke.

COSIN
A Duke art sure? a Duke?

JAQUES
I am sure a Duke,
And so sure, as I know my self for Jaques.

COSIN
Yet the Sun may dazel; Jaques, Was it not
Some leane Commander of an angry Block-house
To keep the Fleemish Eele-boats from invasion,
Or some bold Baron able to dispend
His fifty pounds a year, and meet the foe
Upon the Kings command, in gilded canvas,
And do his deeds of worth? or was it not
Some place of gain, as Clerk to the great Band
Of maribones, that people call the Switzers?
Men made of Beufe, and Sarcenet?

JAQUES

Is a Duke his chamber hung with Nobles like a presence?

COSIN
I am something wavering in my faith;
Would you would settle me, and swear 'tis so,
Is he a Duke indeed?

JAQUES
I swear he is.

COSIN
I am satisfied, he is my Kinsman. Jaques,
And I his poor unworthy Cosin.

JAQUES
True, Sir.

COSIN
I might have been a Duke too, I had means,
A wife as fair as his, and as wise as his;
And could have brookt the Court as well as his,
And laid about her for her husbands honor:
O Jaques, had I ever dreamt of this,
I had prevented him.

JAQUES
Faith Sir it came
Above our expectation, we were wise
Only in seeking to undoe this honor,
Which shewed our dung-hill breeding and our durt.

COSIN
But tell me Jaques,
Why could we not perceive? what dull Divel
Wrought us to cross this noble course, perswading
'Twould be his overthrow? 'fore me a Courtier
Is he that knows all, Jaques, and does all,
'Tis as his noble Grace hath often said,
And very wisely, Jaques, we are fools,
And understand just nothing.

JAQUES
I, as we were, I confess it.
But rising with our great Master,
We shall be call'd to knowledge with our places,
'Tis nothing to be wise, not thus much there,
There's not the least of the billet dealers,
Nor any of the Pastry, or the Kitchin,

But have it in measure delicate.

COSIN
Methinks this greatness of the Dukes my cosins,
(I ask you mercy, Jaques, that near name
Is too familiar for me) should give promise
Of some great benefits to his attendants.

JAQUES
I have a suit my self, and it is sure,
Or I mistake my ends much.

COSIN
What is't Jaques,
May I not crave the place?

JAQUES
Yes, Sir, you shall,
'Tis to be but his Graces Secretary,
Which is my little all, and my ambition,
Till my known worth shall take me by the hand,
And set me higher; how the fates may do
In this poor thread of life, is yet uncertain;
I was not born I take it for a Trencher,
Nor to espouse my Mistriss Dairy-maid.

COSIN
I am resolv'd my Wife shall up to Court;
I'll furnish her, that is a speeding course,
And cannot chuse but breed a mighty fortune;
What a fine youth was I, to let him start,
And get the rise before me! I'll dispatch,
And put my self in Moneys.

JAQUES
Mass 'tis true,
And now you talke of Money; Sir, my business
For taking those Crowns must be dispatcht:
This little plot in the Countrey lies most fit
To do his Grace such serviceable uses,
I must about it.

COSIN
Yet, before you goe,
Give me your hand, and bear my humble service
To the great Duke your Master, and his Duchess,
And live your self in favor: say my Wife
Shall there attend them shortly, so farewell.

JAQUES

I'll see you mounted, Sir.

COSIN

It may not be,

Your place is far above it, spare your self,

And know I am your servant, fare ye well.

[Exit **COSIN**.

JAQUES

Sir I shall rest to be commanded by you,

This place of Secretary will not content me,

I must be more and greater: let me see;

To be a Baron is no such great matter

As people take it: for say I were a Count,

I am still an under-person to this Duke,

Which methinks sounds but harshly: but a Duke?

O I am strangely taken, 'tis a Duke

Or nothing, I'll advise upon't, and see

What may be done by wit and industry.

[Exit.

[Enter **WIFE, LONGOVILE, BEWFORD, SERVANTS.**

WIFE

It must be carried closely with a care

That no man speak unto him, or come near him,

Without our private knowledge, or be made

Afore-hand to our practice:

My good husband,

I shall entreat you now to stay a while,

And prove a noble coxcomb.

Gentlemen,

Your counsel and advice about this carriage.

SERVANT

Alas good man, I do begin to mourn

His dire Massacre: what a persecution

Is pouring down upon him! sure he is sinful.

LONGOVILE

Let him be kept in's chamber under shew

Of state and dignity, and no man suffer'd

To see his noble face, or have access,

But we that are Conspirators.

BEWFORD

Or else down with him into the Countrey amongst his Tenants,
There he may live far longer in his greatness,
And play the fool in pomp amongst his fellows.

WIFE

No, he shall play the fool in the City, and stay,
I will not lose the greatness of this jest,
That shall be given to my wit, for the whole Revenues.

SERVANT

Then thus wee'll have a guard about his person,
That no man come too near him, and our selves
Alwayes in company; have him into the City
To see his face swell; whilst, in divers corners,
Some of our own appointing shall be ready
To cry heaven bless your Grace, long live your Grace.

WIFE

Servant, your counsel's excellent good,
And shall be follow'd, 'twill be rarely strange
To see him stated thus, as though he went
A shroving through the City, or intended
To set up some new stake:
I shall not hold
From open laughter, when I hear him cry,
Come hither my sweet Duchess: let me kiss
Thy gracious lips: for this will be his phrases?
I fear me nothing but his legs will break
Under his mighty weight of such a greatness.

BEWFORD

Now me thinks dearest Lady you are too cruel;
His very heart will freeze in knowing this.

WIFE

No, no, the man was never of such deepness,
To make conceit his Master: Sir, I'll assure ye
He will out-live twenty such pageants.
Were he but my cousin, or my Brother,
And such a desperate killer of his fortune,
In this belief he should dye, though it cost me
A thousand Crowns a day to hold it up;
Or were I not known his wife, and so to have
An equal feeling of this ill he suffers,
He should be thus till all the Boyes i'th' Town
Made sute to weare his badges in their hats,

And walk before his Grace with sticks and nose-gayes,
We Married Women hold—

SERVANT
'Tis well, no more.
The Duke is entring, set your faces right,
And bow like Countrey Prologues: here he comes.
Make room afore, the Duke is entring.

[Enter **DUKE**.

LONGOVILE
The choisest fortunes wait upon our Duke.

SERVANT
And give him all content and happiness.

BEWFORD
Let his great name live to the end of time.

DUKE
We thank you, and are pleas'd to give you notice
We shall at fitter times wait on your Loves,
Till when, be near Us.

LONGOVILE
'Tis a valiant purge, and works extreamly;
'Thas delivered him
Of all Right worshipful and gentle humors,
And left his belly full of nobleness.

DUKE
It pleased the King my Master,
For sundry vertues not unknown to him,
And the all-seeing state, to lend his hand,
And raise me to this Eminence, how this
May seem to other Men, or stir the minds
Of such as are my fellow Peers, I know not,
I would desire their loves in just designs.

WIFE
Now by my faith he does well, very well:
Beshrew my heart I have not seen a better,
Of a raw fellow, that before this day
Never rehearst his state: 'tis marvellous well.

SERVANT
Is he not Duke indeed, see how he looks

As if his spirit were a last, or two
Above his veins, and stretcht his noble hide.

LONGOVILE
Hee's high-brac't like a Drum, pray God he break not.

BEWFORD
Why let him break, there's but a Calves-skin lost.

LONGOVILE
May it please your Grace to see the City,
'Twill be to the minds and much contentment
Of the doubtful people.

DUKE
I am determin'd so, till my return
I leave my honour'd Dutchess to her chamber.
Be careful of your health, I pray you be so.

SERVANT
Your Grace shall suffer us your humble servants
To give attendance, fit so great a person
Upon your body.

DUKE
I am pleased so.

LONGOVILE
Away good Bewford, raise a guard sufficient
To keep him from the reach of Tongues, be quick;
And do you hear, remember how the streets
Must be dispos'd with, for cries, and salutations.
Your Grace determines not to see the King—

DUKE
Not yet, I shall be ready ten dayes hence
To kiss his Highness hand, and give him thanks,
As it is fit I should for his great bounty.
Set forward Gentlemen.

SERVANT
Room for the Duke there.

[Exeunt **DUKE** and **TRAIN**.

WIFE
'Tis fit he should have room to shew his mightiness,
He swells so with his poyson,

'Tis better to reclaim ye thus, than make
A sheeps-head of you, It had been but your due;
But I have mercy Sir, and mean to reclaim you
By a directer course.
That Woman is not worthy of a Soul
That has the sovereign power to rule her husband,
And gives her title up, so long provided
As there be fair play, and his state not wrong'd.

[Enter **SHATTILLION**.

SHATTILLION
I would be glad to know whence this new Duke springs,
The people buz abroad; or by what title
He receiv'd his dignity, 'tis very strange
There should be such close jugling in the State,
But I am ty'd to silence, yet a day
May come, and soon to perfect all these doubts.

WIFE
It is the mad Shattillion by my Soul,
I suffer much for this poor Gentleman;
I'll speak to him, may be he yet knows me.
Monsieur Shattilion.

SHATTILLION
Can you give me reason from whence
This great Duke sprang that walks abroad?

WIFE
Even from the King himself.

SHATTILLION
As you are a Woman, I think you may be cover'd?
Yet your prayer would do no harm good Woman.

WIFE
God preserve him.

[Enter Shattillions' **LOVE**.

SHATTILLION
I say Amen, and so say all good Subjects.

LOVE
Lady, as ever you have lov'd, or shall,
As you have hope of heaven lend your hand,
And wit, to draw this poor distracted man

Under your roofe, from the broad eyes of people,
And wonder of the streets.

WIFE
With all my heart;
My feeling of his grief and loss is much.

LOVE
Sir, now you are come so near the prison, will ye
Goe in, and visit your fair Love: poor soul
She would be glad to see you.

SHATTILLION
This same Duke is but
Apocryphal, there's no creation
That can stand where titles are not right.

LOVE
'Tis true, Sir.

SHATTILLION
That is another draught upon my life;
Let me examine well the words I spake.
The words I spake were, that this novel Duke
Is not o'th' true making, 'tis to me most certain.

WIFE
You are as right, Sir, as you went by line.

SHATTILLION
And to the grief of many thousands more.

WIFE
If there be any such, God comfort them.

SHATTILLION
Whose mouths may open when the time shall please;
I'm betray'd, commend me to the King,
And tell him I am sound, and crave but justice;
You shall not need to have your guard upon me,
Which I am sure are plac'd for my attachment;
Lead on; I'm obedient to my bonds.

LOVE
Good Sir be not displeased with us;
We are but servants to his Highness will,
To make that good.

SHATTILLION
I do forgive you even with my heart;
Shall I entreat a favor?

WIFE
Any thing.

SHATTILLION
To see my love before that fatal stroak,
And publish to the world my christian death,
And true obedience to the Crown of France.

LOVE
I hope it shall not need Sir, for there is mercy
As well as Justice in his Royal heart.

[Exeunt.

[Enter **THREE GENTLEMEN**.

FIRST GENTLEMAN
Every man take his corner, here am I,
You there, and you in that place, so be perfect,
Have a great care your cries be loud; and faces
Full of dejected fear and humbleness.
He comes.

[Enter **JAQUES**.

JAQUES
Fye, how these streets are charg'd and swell'd
With these same rascally people! give more room,
Or I shall have occasion to distribute
A martial almes amongst you; as I am a Gentleman
I have not seen such rude disorder,
They follow him like a prize, there's no true gaper
Like to your Citizen, he will be sure
The Beares shall not pass by his door in peace,
But he and all his family will follow.
Room there afore: Sound:

[Enter **DUKE** and his **COMPANY**.

JAQUES
Give room, and keep your places, you may see enough; keep your places.

LONGOVILE
These people are too far unmanner'd, thus

To stop your Graces way with multitudes.

DUKE
Rebuke them not, good Monsieur, 'tis their loves
Which I will answer, if it please my stars
To spare me life and health.

SECOND GENTLEMAN
Bless your Grace.

DUKE
And you with all my heart.

FIRST GENTLEMAN
Now heaven preserve your happy dayes:

DUKE
I thank you too.

THIRD GENTLEMAN
Now Heaven save your Grace;

DUKE
I thank you all.

BEWFORD
On there before.

DUKE
Stand Gentlemen, stay yet a while.
For I am minded to impart my love
To these good people, and my friends,
Whose love and prayers for my greatness,
Are equal in abundance, note me well,
And with my words; my heart? for as the Tree—

LONGOVILE
Your Grace had best beware, 'twill be inform'd
Your greatness with the people.

DUKE
I had more,
My honest, and ingenious people.—But
The weight of business hath prevented me.
I am call'd from you: but this tree I spake of
Shall bring forth fruit, I hope, to your content,
And so I share my bowels amongst you all.

OMNES
A noble Duke, a very noble Duke.

[Enter a **GENTLEMAN**.

SERVANT
Afore there Gentlemen.

GENTLEMAN
You'r faithfully met good Monsieur Mount Marine.

SERVANT
Be advis'd, the time is alter'd.

GENTLEMAN
Is he not the same man he was afore?

DUKE
Still the same man to you, Sir.

LONGOVILE
You have received mighty Grace, be thankful.

GENTLEMAN
Let me not dye in ignorance;

LONGOVILE
You shall not.
Then know, the King out of his love, hath pleas'd
To stile him Duke of Burgundy.

GENTLEMAN
O great Duke,
Thus low, I plead for pardon, and desire
To be enrol'd amongst your poorest slaves.

DUKE
Sir, you have mercy, and withal my hand,
From henceforth let me call you one of mine.

SERVANT
Make room afore there, and dismiss the people.

DUKE
Every Man to his house in peace and quiet.

SERVANT
Now heaven preserve the Duke, heaven bless the Duke.

[Exeunt **OMNES**.

[Enter **WIFE**.

WIFE
This Letter came this morn from my Cosin
To the great Lady, high and mighty Duchess
Of Burgundy, be these delivered. Oh,
For a stronger lace to keep my breath
That I may laugh the nine days till the wonder
Fall to an ebb: the high and mighty Duchess?
The high and mighty God? what a stile is this!
Methinks it goes like a Duchy lope-man,
A ladder of 100 rounds will fail
To reach the top on't: well my gentle Cosin
I know by these contents, your itch of honor;
You must to the Court you say, and very shortly:
You shall be welcome; and if your wife have wit
I'll put her in a thriving course, if not
Her own sin on her own head, not a blot
Shall stain my reputation, only this
I must for healths sake sometimes make an ass
Of the tame moil my Husband; 'twill do him good,
And give him fresher brains, Me fresher bloud.
Now for the noble Duke, I hear him coming.

[Enter **DUKE**, his **TRAIN**.

Your Grace is well return'd.

DUKE
As well as may be:
Never in younger health, never more able:
I mean to be your bed-fellow this night,
Let me have good encounter.

BEWFORD
Bless me heaven
What a hot meat this greatness is!

LONGOVILE
It may be so,
For I'll be sworn he hath not got a snap
This two months on my knowledge, or her woman
Is damn'd for swearing it.

DUKE

I thank you Gentlemen for your attendance
And also your great pains, pray know my Lodgings
Better and oftner, do so Gentlemen.
Now by my honor, as I am a Prince,
I speak sincerely, know my lodgings better,
And be not strangers, I shall see your service
And your deservings, when you least expect.

OMNES
We humbly thank your grace for this great favor.

DUKE
Jaques?

JAQUES
Your Grace.

DUKE
Be ready for the Countrey,
And let my Tenants know the Kings great love:
Say I would see them, but the weight at Court
Lies heavy on my shoulders: let them know
I do expect their duties in attendance
Against the next feast, wait for my coming
To take up Post-horse, and be full of speed.

[Exit **JAQUES**.

WIFE
I would desire your Grace—

DUKE
You shall desire, and have your
Full desire: sweet Duchess speak.

WIFE
To have some conference with a Gentleman
That seems not altogether void of reason.
He talks of Titles, and things near the Crown,
And knowing none so fit as your good Grace,
To give the difference in such points of State—

DUKE
What is he? if he be noble, or have any part
That's worthy our converse, we do accept him.

WIFE
I can assure your Grace, his strain is noble,

But he's very subtle.

DUKE
Let him be so.
Let him have all the brains, I shall demonstrate
How this most Christian Crown of France can bear
No other shew of Title than the Kings.
I will go in and meditate for half an hour,
And then be ready for him presently,
I will convert him quickly, or confound him.

SERVANT
Is mad Shattillion here?

WIFE
Is here, and's Lady,
I prethee servant fetch him hither.

SERVANT
Why, what do you mean to put him to?

WIFE
To chat with the mad lad my Husband;
'Twill be brave to hear them speak, babble,
Stare, and prate.

BEWFORD
But what shall be the end of all this, Lady?

[Enter **SHATTILLION** and **LADY**.

WIFE
Leave that to me, now for the grand dispute,
For see, here comes Shattillion: as I live, methinks
All France should bear part of his griefs.

LONGOVILE
I'll fetch my Lord the Duke.

SHATTILLION
Where am I now, or whether will you lead me?
To my death? I crave my priviledge,
I must not dye, but by just course of Law.

SERVANT
His Majesty hath sent by me your pardon,
He meant not you should dye; but would intreat you
To lay the full state of your Title open,

Unto a grave and Noble Gentleman.

[Enter **DUKE** and **LONGOVILE**.

The Duke of Burgundy who here doth come,
Who, either by his wisdom will confute you,
Or else inform and satisfie the King.

BEWFORD
May't please your grace, this is the Gentleman.

DUKE
Is this he that chops Logick with my Liege?

SHATTILLION
D'ye mock me? you are great, the time will come,
When you shall be as much contemn'd as I,
Where are the antient compliments of France,
The upstarts brave the Princes of the bloud?

DUKE
Your Title Sir, in short.

SHATTILLION
He must Sir,
Be a better States-man than your self, that can
Trip me in any thing, I will not speak
Before these witnesses.

DUKE
Depart the room, for none shall stay,
No, not my dearest Duchess.

WIFE
We'll stand behind the Arras and hear all.

[Exeunt.

DUKE
In that chair take your place, I in this,
Discourse your Title now.

SHATTILLION
Sir, you shall know,
My Loves true Title, mine by Marriage,
Setting aside the first race of French Kings,
Which will not here concern us, as Pharamond,
With Clodian, Meroveus, and Chilperick,

And to come down unto the second Race,
Which we will likewise slip—

DUKE
But take me with you.

SHATTILLION
I pray you give me leave, of Martel Charles,
The Father of King Pippin, who was, Sire
To Charles the Great, and famous Charlemain.
And to come to the third Race of French Kings,
Which will not be greatly pertinent in this cause,
Betwixt the King and me, of which you know
HUGH CAPET was the first,
Next his Son Robert, Henry then, and Philip
With Lewis, and his Son a Lewis too,
And of that name the Seventh, but all this
Springs from a Female, as it shall appear.

DUKE
Now give me leave, I grant you this your Title
At the first sight, carries some shew of truth;
But if ye weigh it well, ye shall find light.
Is not his Majesty possest in peace,
And justice executed in his name,
And can you think the most Christian King
Would do this if he saw not reason for it?

SHATTILLION
But had not the Tenth Lewis a sole Daughter?

DUKE
I cannot tell.

SHATTILLION
But answer me directly.

DUKE
It is a most seditious question.

SHATTILLION
Is this your justice?

DUKE
I stand for my King.

SHATTILLION
Was ever Heir-apparant thus abus'd?

I'll have your head for this.

DUKE
Why, do your worst.

SHATTILLION
Will no one stir to apprehend this Traitor?
A guard about my person, will none come?
Must my own royal hands perform the deed?
Then thus I do arrest you.

DUKE
Treason, help.

[Enter **WIFE, LONGOVILE, BEWFORD** and **SERVANT**.

WIFE
Help, help, my Lord and Husband.

DUKE
Help the Duke.

LONGOVILE
Forbear his grace's person.

SHATTILLION
Forbear you to touch him that
Your Heir-apparent weds,
But by this hand, I will have all your heads.

[Exit.

SERVANT
How doth your Grace?

DUKE
Why? well.

SERVANT
How do you find his Title?

DUKE
'Tis a dangerous one,
As can come by a female.

SERVANT
I, 'tis true,
But the Law Salique cuts him off from all.

LONGOVILE
I do beseech your Grace, how stands his Title?

DUKE
Pew, nothing; the Law Salique cuts him off from all.

WIFE
My gracious Husband, you must now prepare,
In all your Graces pomp to entertain
Your Cosin, who is now a convertite,
And follows here, this night he will be here.

DUKE
Be ready all in haste, I do intend,
To shew before my Cosin's wondring face,
The greatness of my pomp, and of my place.

[Exeunt **OMNES**.

ACTUS QUARTUS

SCÆNA PRIMA

Enter **COSIN** and his **WIFE**.

COSIN
Sirrah, is all things carried to the Tailor?
The measure, and the fashion of the Gown,
With the best trim?

WIFE
Yes Sir, and 'twill be ready within this two days.

COSIN
For my self I care not,
I have a suit or two of antient Velvet;
Which with some small correcting and addition,
May steal into the presence.

WIFE
Would my Gown were ready; Husband, I'll lay my life,
To make you something e'r to morrow night.

COSIN
It must not be

Before we see the Duke, and have advice,
How to behave our selves: lets in the while,
And keep our selves from knowledge, till time shall call us.

[Enter **LONGOVILE** and **BEWFORD**.

LONGOVILE
I much admire the fierce masculine spirit,
Of this dread Amazon.

BEWFORD
This following night I'll have a wench in solace.

LONGOVILE
Sir, I hear you,
And will be with you if I live, no more.

[Enter **MARIA**.

MARIA
My Lady would intreat your presence, Gentlemen.

BEWFORD
We will obey your Lady, she is worthy.

LONGOVILE
You, light alone, a word, or two.

MARIA
Your Will, Sir.

LONGOVILE
Hark in your ear; wilt thou be married? speak, wilt thou marry?

MARIA
Married? to whom Sir?

LONGOVILE
To a proper fellow, landed, and able bodied.

MARIA
Why do you flout me, Sir?

LONGOVILE
I swear I do not; I love thee for thy Ladies sake, be free?

MARIA
If I could meet such matches as you speak of,

I were a very child to lose my time, Sir.

LONGOVILE
What saist thou to Monsieur Bewford?

MARIA
Sir, I say he's a proper Gentleman, and far
Above my means to look at.

LONGOVILE
Dost thou like him?

MARIA
Yes Sir, and ever did.

LONGOVILE
He is thine own.

MARIA
You are too great in promises.

LONGOVILE
Be rul'd, and follow my advice, he shall be thine.

MARIA
Would you would make it good, Sir.

LONGOVILE
Do but thus,
Get thee a cushion underneath thy cloaths,
And leave the rest to me.

MARIA
I'll be your scholar,
I cannot lose much by the venture sure.

LONGOVILE
Thou wilt lose a pretty maidenhead, my rogue,
Or I am much o'th' bow hand, you'll remember
If all this take effect, who did it for you,
And what I may deserve for such a kindness.

MARIA
Yours Sir.

[Exeunt.

[Enter **JAQUES** and **SHATTILLION** severally.

JAQUES
Save ye Sir.

SHATTILLION
Save the King.

JAQUES
I pray you Sir, which is the nearest way.

SHATTILLION
Save the King, this is the nearest way.

JAQUES
Which is the nearest way to the Post-house?

SHATTILLION
God save the King and his Post-house.

JAQUES
I pray Sir direct me to the house.

SHATTILLION
Heaven save the King, you cannot catch me, Sir.

JAQUES
I do not understand you, Sir.

SHATTILLION
You do not, I say you cannot catch me, Sir.

JAQUES
Not catch you, Sir?

SHATTILLION
No Sir, nor can the King,
With all his stratagems, and his forced tricks,
Although he put his Nobles in disguise;
Never so oft to sift into my words,
By course of Law, lay hold upon my life.

JAQUES
It is business that my Lord the Duke
Is by the King imployed in, and he thinks
I am acquainted with it.

SHATTILLION
I shall not need to rip the cause up,

From the first, to you,
But if his Majesty had suffer'd me
To marry her, though she be after him,
The right heir general to the Crown of France.
I would not have convey'd her into Spain,
As it was thought, nor would I e'er have joyn'd,
With the reformed Churches, to make them,
Stand for my cause.

JAQUES
I do not think you would.

SHATTILLION
I thank you Sir,
And since I see you are a favourer
Of virtues, kept in bondage;
Tell directly to my soveraign King,
For so I will acknowledge him for ever,
How you have found my staid affections
Setled for peace, and for the present state.

JAQUES
Why Sir?

SHATTILLION
And good Sir, tell him further this,
That notwithstanding all suggestions
Brought to him against me, and all his suspitions,
Which are innumerable to my treasons,
If he will warrant me but publique trial,
I'll freely yeild my self into his hands;
Can he have more than this?

JAQUES
No by my troth.

SHATTILLION
I would his Majesty would hear but reason,
As well as you.

JAQUES
But Sir, you do mistake me,
For I never saw the King.
In all my life but once, therefore good Sir,
May it please you to shew me which is the Post-house.

SHATTILLION
I cry you mercy, Sir, then you are my friend.

JAQUES
Yes Sir.

SHATTILLION
And such men are very rare with me,
The Post-house is hard by, farewel;

JAQUES
I thank you, Sir, I must ride hard to night,
And it is dark already.

SHATTILLION
I am cruel, to send this man directly to his death
That is my friend, and I might easily save him,
He shall not dye, come back, my friend, come back.

JAQUES
What is your Will?

SHATTILLION
Do you not know?

JAQUES
Not I.

SHATTILLION
And do you gather nothing by my face?

JAQUES
No Sir.

SHATTILLION
Virtue is ever innocent,
Lay not the fault on me, I grieve for you,
And wish that all my tears might win your safety.

JAQUES
Why Sir?

SHATTILLION
Alas good friend you are undone,
The more ill fortune, mine to be the means
Of your sad overthrow, you know not me.

JAQUES
No truly Sir.

SHATTILLION
Would you had never seen me,
I am a man pursu'd by the whole state
And sure some one hath seen me talk with you.

JAQUES
Yes, divers Sir.

SHATTILLION
Why then your head is gone.

JAQUES
I'll out of town.

SHATTILLION
Would it were soon enough,
Stay if you love your life, or else you are taken.

JAQUES
What shall I do?

SHATTILLION
I'll venture deeply for him,
Rather than to cast away an innocent,
Take courage friend, I will preserve thy life,
With hazard of mine own.

JAQUES
I thank you, Sir.

SHATTILLION
This night thou shalt be lodg'd within my doors,
Which shall be all lock'd fast, and in the morn
I'll so provide, you shall have free access,
To the Sea-side, and so be shipt away,
E'r any know it.

JAQUES
Good Sir, suddainly, I am afraid to dye.

SHATTILLION
Then follow me.

[Exeunt.

[Enter Shatillion's **LOVE**.

LOVE

This way he went, and there's the house, I hope,
His better Angel hath directed him,
To leave the wandring streets, poor Gentleman.
Would I were able with as free a heart,
To set his soul right, as I am to grieve,
The ruine of his fame, which God forgive me;
Sir, if you be within, I pray Sir speak to me.

SHATTILLION
I am within, and will be; what are you?

LOVE
A friend.

SHATTILLION
No Sir, you must pardon me,
I am acquainted with none such: be speedy,
Friend, there is no other remedy.

LOVE
A word Sir, I say, I am your friend.

SHATTILLION
You cannot scape by any other means,
Be not fearful, God save the King,
What's your business, Sir?

LOVE
To speak with you.

SHATTILLION
Speak out then.

LOVE
Shall I not come up?

SHATTILLION
Thou shalt not: flie if thou be'st thine own friend,
There lies the suit and all the furniture
Belonging to the head, on with it friend.

LOVE
Sir do you hear?

SHATTILLION
I do, God bless the King,
It was a habit I had laid aside,
For my own person, if the state had forced me.

LOVE
Good Sir, unlock your door.

SHATTILLION
Be full of speed, I see some 20 Musquetiers in ambush
Whate'r thou art, know I am here and will be,
Seest thou this bloody sword that cries revenge?
Shake not my friend, through millions of these foes
I'll be thy guard, and set thee safe aboard.

LOVE
Dare you not trust me, Sir?

SHATTILLION
My good sword before me,
And my allegeance to the King I tell thee
Captain (for so I ghess thee by thy Arms)
And the loose flanks of Halberdiers about thee,
Thou art too weak, and foolish to attempt me.
If you be ready, follow me, and hark you
Upon your life speak to no living wight,
Except my self.

LOVE
Monsieur Shattillion?

SHATTILLION
Thou shalt not call agen; thus with my sword,
And the strong faith I bear unto the King;
Whom God preserve, I will descend my chamber,
And cut thy throat, I swear I'll cut thy throat,
Steal after me and live.

LOVE
I will not stay.
The fury of a man so far distracted.

[Exit **LOVE**.

SHATTILLION
Where's the Officer that dares not enter,
To intrap the life of my distressed friend?
I, have you hid your self? you must be found,
What do you fear? is not authority on your side
Nay, I know the Kings command
Will be your warrant, why then fear you? speak
What strange designs are these? Shattillion,

Be resolute and bear thy self upright,
Though the whole world despise thee: soft, methinks.
I heard a rushing which was like the shake
Of a discovered Officer, I'll search
The whole street over, but I'll find thee out.

[Exit.

[Enter **JAQUES** in womans apparel.

JAQUES
How my joynts do shake, where had I been
But for this worthy Gentleman, that
Hath some touch of my infortunes; would I were
Safe under hatches once, for Callicut,
Farewel the pomp of Court, I never more
Can hope to be a Duke or any thing,
I never more shall see the glorious face
Of my fair spreading Lord that lov'd me well.

[Enter **SHATTILLION**.

SHATTILLION
Fly you so fast? I had a sight of you,
But would not follow you; I was too wise,
You shall not lead me with a cunning trick;
Where you may catch me; poor Shattillion;
Hath the Kings anger left thee never a friend?
No, all mens loves move by the breath of Kings.

JAQUES
It is the Gentleman that sav'd my life, Sir.

SHATTILLION
Bless Shattillion, another plot.

JAQUES
No Sir, 'tis I.

SHATTILLION
Why, who are you?

JAQUES
Your friend whom you preserv'd.

SHATTILLION
Whom I preserv'd?
My friend? I have no woman friend but one,

Who is too close in prison to be here;
Come near, let me look on you.

JAQUES
'Tis I.

SHATTILLION
You should not be a woman by your stature.

JAQUES
I am none, Sir.

SHATTILLION
I know it, then keep off,
Strange men and times! how I am still preserv'd!
Here they have sent a yeoman of the guard,
Disguis'd in womans clothes, to work on me,
To make love to me; and to trap my words,
And so insnare my life, I know you, Sir,
Stand back, upon your peril, can this be
In Christian Common-weals, from this time forth
I'll cut off all the means to work on me,
I'll ne'er stir from my house: and keep my doors
Lockt day and night, and cheapen meat and drink
At the next shops by Signs, out of my window,
And having bought it, draw it up in my garters.

JAQUES
Sir, will you help me?

SHATTILLION
Do not follow me,
I'll take a course to live, despight of men.

[Exit **SHATTILLION**.

JAQUES
He dares not venture for me, wretched Jaques!
Thou art undone for ever and for ever,
Never to rise again? what shall I do?

[Enter **BEWFORT**.

Where shall I hide me? here's one to take me,
I must stand close, and not speak for my life.

BEWFORD
This is the time of night, and this the haunt,

In which I use to catch my Wastcoatiers,
It is not very dark, no, I shall spie 'em,
I have walk't out in such a pitchy night.
I could not see my fingers this far off,
And yet have brought home venison by the smell,
I hope they have not left their old walk, ah?
Have I spied you sitting by this light?
To me there's no such fine sight in the world,
As a white apron 'twixt twelve and one;
See how it glisters! do you think to scape?
See now I have you fast; come, and do not strive,
It takes away the edge of appetite;
Come, I'll be liberal every way.
Take heed you make no noise, for waking of the Watch.

[Exeunt.

[Enter **COSIN** and his **WIFE**.

COSIN
Now the blessing of some happy guide,
To bring us to the Duke, and we are ready.

[Enter **LONGOVILE** and **SERVANT**.

Come forward, see the door is open'd,
And two of his Gentlemen
I'll speak to them,
And mark how I behave my self, God save ye;
For less I cannot wish to men of sort, and of your seeming:
Are you of the Dukes?

LONGOVILE
We are, Sir, and your servants, your salutes,
We give you back again with many thanks.

COSIN
When did you hear such words before Wife? peace,
Do you not dare to answer yet; is't fit
So mean a Gentleman as my self should crave,
The presence of the great Duke your Master?

SERVANT
Sir you may.

LONGOVILE
Shall we desire your name, and business, Sir?
And we will presently inform him of you.

COSIN
My name is Cleremont.

SERVANT
You are his Graces kinsman,
Or I am much mistaken?

COSIN
You are right,
Some of his noble bloud runs through these veins,
Though far unworthy of his graces knowledge.

LONGOVILE
Sir, we must all be yours; his graces kinsman,
And we so much forgetful? 'twas a rudeness,
And must attend your pardon, thus I crave it:
First to this beauteous Lady, whom I take
To be your Wife, Sir, next your mercy.

COSIN
You have it, Sir, I do not like this kissing,
It lies so open to a world of wishes.

SERVANT
This is the merry fellow; this is he
That must be noble too.

LONGOVILE
And so he shall.
If all the Art I have can make him noble,
I'll dub him with a Knight-hood; if his wife
Will be but forward, and joyn issue,
I like her above excellent.

SERVANT
Wil't please you
To walk a turn or two, whilst to the Duke
We make your comming known?

[Exit **SERVANT** and **LONGOVILE**.

COSIN
I shall attend, Sir.

WIFE
These Gentlemen are very proper men,
And kiss the best that e'er I tasted.

For goodness-sake husband, let us never more
Come near the Countrey, whatsoe'er betide us;
I am in malice with the memory
Of that same stinking dung-hil.

COSIN
Why now you are my chicken and my dear,
Love where I love, hate where I hate: now
You shall have twenty Gowns, and twenty Chains,
See, the door is opening.

SERVANT
Room afore there, the Duke is entring.

[Enter **DUKE**, **DUCHESS**, **LONGOVILE**, **SERVANT**, **MARIA**.

COSIN
'Tis the Duke, even he himself, be merry,
This is the golden age the Poet speaks on.

WIFE
I pray it be not brazen'd by their faces,
And yet methinks they are the neatest Pieces
For shape, and cutting that e'er I beheld.

COSIN
Most gracious Duke, my poor Spouse and my self,
Do kiss your mighty foot, and next to that
The great hand of your Dutchess, ever wishing
Your honors ever springing, and your years.

DUKE
Cosin?

COSIN
Your Graces vassal, far unworthy
The nearness of your blood.

DUKE
Correct me not, I know the word I speak,
And know the person.
Though I be something higher than the place
Where common men have motion, and descending
Down with my eye, their forms are lessened to me;
Yet from this pitch can I behold my own,
From millions of those men that have no mark,
And in my fearful stoop, can make them stand,
When others feel my feet, and perish: Cosin,

Be comforted, you are very welcome, so
Is your fair Wife: the charge of whom I give
To my own dearest, and best beloved.
Tell me, you have resolv'd your self for Court,
And utterly renounc'd the slavish Countrey,
With all the cares thereof?

COSIN
I have, Sir.

DUKE
Have you dismist your eating houshold,
Sold your hangings of Nebuchadnezar, for such they were,
As I remember, with the Furnitures
Belonging to your Beds and Chambers?

COSIN
I Sir.

DUKE
Have you most carefully ta'en off the Lead,
From your roof, weak with age, and so prevented
The ruin of your house, and clapt him
In a summer suit of thatch to keep him cool?

COSIN
All this I have perform'd.

DUKE
Then lend me all your hands, I will embrace my Cosin
Who is an understanding Gentleman,
And with a zeal mighty, as is my name,
Once more I bid you welcome to the Court;
My state again.

DUCHESS
As I was telling you, your Husband
Must be no more Commander, look to that,
Be several at meat, and lodging, let him have
Board-wages, and Diet, 'mongst his men i'th' Town
For pleasure, if he be given to't, let him have it,
Else as your own fancy shall direct you.
Cosin, you see this mighty man here: he was an ass
When he came first to Town: indeed he was
Just such another coxcomb as your Husband,
God bless the mark, and every good mans child!
This must not stir you Cosin.

WIFE
Heaven forbid!

LONGOVILE
Sweet Maria; provide the cushion ready for it.

MARIA
It shall be done.

DUKE
Receive all your advices from our self,
Be once a day with us, and so farewel
For this time, my fair Cosin, Gentlemen
Conduct him to his Lodging.

DUCHESS
Farewel, and think upon my words.

WIFE
I shall observe them.

[Exit **DUKE** and **DUCHESS**.

COSIN
Health, and the Kings continual love, attend you.

SERVANT
Oh for a private place to ease my Lungs!
Heaven give me patience, such a pair of jades
Were never better ridden to this hour,
Pray heaven they hold out to the journeys end.

LONGOVILE
Twitch him aside good Monsieur, whilst I break
Upon the body of his strength, his wife,
I have a constant promise: she is my own.

SERVANT
Ply her to wind-ward Monsieur, you have taken
The most compendious way to raise your self,
That could have been delivered by a Counsel.

COSIN
I have some certain aims, Sir: but my wife—

SERVANT
Your wife, you must not let that trouble you.

COSIN

It will Sir, to see her in a strangers arms.

SERVANT

What mean you? let her alone, be wise, stir not a foot
For if you do, all your hopes are buried:
I swear you are a lost man if you stir.

COSIN

I thank you Sir, I will be more advis'd.

SERVANT

But what great Office do you level at?

COSIN

Sir, they are kissing.

SERVANT

Let them kiss,
And much may do their good hearts; they must kiss
And kiss, and double kiss, and kiss again,
Or you may kiss the post for any rising:
Had your noble kinsman ever mounted
To these high Spheres of honor, now he moves in,
But for the kisses of his wife?

COSIN

I know not.

SERVANT

Then I do; credit me, he had been lost,
A fellow of no mark, and no repute.
Had not his wife kist soon, and very sweetly:
She was an excellent woman, and dispatcht him
To his full being, in a moment, Sir—

[Exit **LONGOVILE** and **WIFE**.

COSIN

But yet methinks he should not take her, Sir,
Into a private room.

SERVANT

Now stand and flourish,
You are a made man for ever.
I do envy you if you stand your fortunes up,
You are the happiest man, but your great Cosin,
This day in Court: well, I will marry surely,

And not let every man out-run me thus.
'Tis time to be mine own friend, I live
In town here, and direct the readiest way,
To other men, and be a slave my self.

COSIN
Nay, good Sir be not mov'd, I am your servant,
And will not be ungrateful for this knowledge.

SERVANT
Will you be walking home?

COSIN
I would desire to have my wife along.

SERVANT
You are too raw,
Begone, and take no notice where you left her,
Let her return at leasure, if she stay
A month, 'twill be the better, understand me
This Gentleman can do't.

COSIN
I will Sir, and wife remember me, a Duke, a Duke wife.

[Exit **COSIN**.

SERVANT
Aboard her Longovile, she's thine own,
To me the fooling of this fool is venery.

[Exit **SERVANT**.

[Enter **BEWFORD** and **JAQUES**.

BEWFORD
Come, prethee come, have I not crowns? behold
And follow me, here; not a word, go in
Grope by the walls, and you shall find a bed,
Lie down there, see, see, a turn or two, to give
My blood some heats, and I am presently
For action: darkness, by thy leave, I come.

[Exit **BEWFORD**.

[Enter **MARIA**.

MARIA

I am perfect in my lesson, be my speed,
Thou god of marriage, this is the door, I'll knock.

BEWFORD [within]
Whose there, I cannot come yet.

MARIA
Monsieur Bewford?

BEWFORD
Stay till I light a candle, who are ye?

MARIA
Sir? a poor Gentlewoman.

[Enter **BEWFORD**.

BEWFORD
Oh come in, I'll find a time for you too, be not loud.

MARIA
Sir, you have found that time already, shame
On my soul therefore.

BEWFORD
Why? what's the matter?

MARIA
Do you not see, Sir, is your light so dim?

BEWFORD
Do you not wait on the Lady Mount Marine?

MARIA
I do Sir, but my love on you.

BEWFORD
Poor soul! how cam'st thou by this big belly?

MARIA
By your self.

BEWFORD
By heaven I ne'er touch'd your body.

MARIA
Yes, unswear that oath again, I'll tell you all;
These two years I have lov'd you, but the means

How to enjoy you, I did never know
Till Twelf-night last, when hearing of your game
To take up wenches private in the night,
I apprehended straight this course to make
My self as one of them, and wait your coming;
I did so, and enjoyed you, and now this child
That now is quick within me, hide my shame,
And marry me, or else I must be forc'd—

LONGOVILE [within]
Monsieur Bewford, Monsieur Bewford.

BEWFORD
Whose that calls?

LONGOVILE
Are you a bed?

BEWFORD
No Sir, the hangings.

[Enter **LONGOVILE**.

LONGOVILE
Nay Monsieur, I'll forbid that, we'll have fair play,
Lend me your candle, are you taken Bewford?
A lecher of your practice, and close carriage
To be discovered thus? I am asham'd
So great a master in his art should fail,
And stagger in his grounds.

BEWFORD
You're wide,
This woman and my self are man and wife,
And have been so this half year,
Where are you now? have I been discover'd?
You cannot break so easily on me, Sir,
I am too wary to be open'd by you.

LONGOVILE
But these are but illusions, to give colour
To your most mystick leachery, but Sir,
The belly hath betraid you all, it must out.

BEWFORD
Good Longovile believe me on my faith,
I am her husband.

LONGOVILE

On my faith I cannot, unless I saw
Your hands fast, and your hearts.

BEWFORD

Why Longovile, when did I give that to your ears,
That was not truth? by all the world she's mine,
She is my wife, and to confirm you better
I give my self again, here take my hand
And I yours, we are once more married,
Will this content you?

LONGOVILE

Yes I am believing, and God give you joy.

BEWFORD

My loving wife, I will not wrong thee,
Since I am thine and only loved of thee
From this hour I vow my self a new man,
Be not jealous: for though I had a purpose,
To have spent an hour or two in solace otherwise,
And was provided for it, yet my love
Shall put a better temper to my blood,
Come out thou woman of unwholsome life,
Be sorry for thy sins, and learn to mend,
Nay, never hide your face, you shall be seen.

LONGOVILE

Jaques, why Jaques, art thou that Jaques,
The very staffe, and right hand of our Duke?
Speak, thou bearded Venus.

JAQUES

I am he, by miracle preserv'd to be that Jaques,
Within this two hours Gentlemen, poor Jaques
Was but as coarse in grave: a man of wisdom,
That of my conscience, if he had his right
Should have a pretty State, but that's all one
That Noble Gentleman did save this life,
I keep it for him, 'tis his own.

LONGOVILE

Oh Bacchus! is all the world drunk? come we'll to the Duke
And give thanks for this delivery.

ACTUS QUINTUS

Enter **DUKE** and **JAQUES**.

DUKE
Not gone unto my Tenants to relate
My Grace and Honor; and the mightiness
Of my new name, which would have struck a terror
Through their course doublets, to their very hearts?

JAQUES
Alas, great Lord and Master, I could scarce
With safety of my life return again
Unto your graces house, and but for one
That had some mercy, I had sure been hang'd.

DUKE
My house?

JAQUES
Yes Sir, this house, your house i' th' Town.

DUKE
Jaques we are displeas'd, hath it no name?

JAQUES
What name?

DUKE
Dull rogue; what hath the King bestow'd
So many honors, open'd all his springs,
And show'red his graces down upon my head,
And has my house no name? no title yet?
Burgundy house you ass.

JAQUES
Your graces mercy,
when I was come off, and had recover'd
Burgundy house, I durst not yet be seen,
But lay all night for fear of pursevants
In Burgundy privie house.

DUKE
Oh Sir, 'tis well,
Can you remember now? but Jaques know
Since thy intended journey is so crost,
I will go down my self this morning.

JAQUES
Sir?

DUKE
Have I not said this morning?

JAQUES
But consider,
That nothing is prepared yet for your journey,
Your graces teams not here to draw your cloaths;
And not a Carrier yet in town to send by.

DUKE
I say once more go about it,
You're a wise man, you'd have me linger time,
Till I have worn these cloaths out: will ye go?

[Exit **JAQUES**.

Make ye ready Wife.

[Enter **DUCHESS**.

DUCHESS
I am so, mighty Duke.

DUKE
Nay, for the Countrey.

DUCHESS
How? for the Countrey?

DUKE
Yes I am resolv'd to see my Tenants in this bravery,
Make them a sumptuous feast, with a slight shew,
Of Dives and Lazarus, and a squib or two,
And so return.

DUCHESS
Why Sir? you are not mad?

DUKE
How many Dukes have ye known mad? I pray speak.

DUCHESS
You are the first, Sir, and I hope the last,
But you are stark horn-mad.

DUKE
Forbear good wife.

DUCHESS
As I have faith you're mad: your horns
Have been too heavy for you, and have broke
Your skull in pieces: If you be in earnest.

DUKE
Well, you shall know my skull and wits are whole
E'r I have done, and yet I am in earnest.

DUCHESS
Why, do you think I'll go?

DUKE
I know you shall.

DUCHESS
I shall? by what authority shall I?

DUKE
I am your Husband.

DUCHESS
True, I confess it,
And by that name, the world hath given you
A power to sway me; but Sir, you shall know
There is a greater bond that ties me here,
Allegeance to the King, has he not heapt
Those honors on you to no other end,
But to stay you here, and shall I have a hand
In the offending such a gracious Prince?
Besides, our own undoings lies upon't,
Were there no other cause, I do not see,
Why you should go: If I should say you should not.

DUKE
Do you think so?

DUCHESS
Yes faith.

DUKE
Now good wife make me understand that point.

DUCHESS

Why that you shall, did I not bring you hither?

DUKE
Yes.

DUCHESS
And were not all these honors wrought out of the fire by me?

DUKE
By you?

DUCHESS
By me? how strange you make it!
When you came first, did you not walk the Town,
In a long Cloak half compass? an old Hat,
Lin'd with Vellure, and on it for a band,
A skein of crimson Cruil?

DUKE
I confess it.

DUCHESS
And took base courses?

DUKE
Base?

DUCHESS
Base, by this light, extream base, and scurvie, monstrous base.

DUKE
What were these courses, wife?

DUCHESS
Why, you shall know,
Did you not thus attir'd, trot up and down,
Plotting for vild and lowsie Offices,
And agreed with the Sergeant of the Bears,
To buy his place? deny this, if you can.

DUKE
Why it is true.

DUCHESS
And was not that monstrous base?

DUKE
Be advis'd wife, a Bear's a Princely beast.

DUCHESS
A Bear?

DUKE
Yes wife, and one side venison.

DUCHESS
You're more than one side fool, I'm sure of that.

DUKE
But since you have vext me wife, know you shall go;
Or you shall never have penny from me.

DUCHESS
Nay, I have done, and though I know 'twill be
Your overthrow, I'll not forsake you now.

DUKE
Be ready then.

[Exit **DUKE**.

DUCHESS
I will.

[Enter **BEWFORD**, **LONGOVILE**, **SERVANT**, **MARIA**.

LONGOVILE
What are you married Bewford?

BEWFORD
I, as fast as words, and hearts, and hands, and Priest can make us.

DUCHESS
Oh Gentlemen, we are undone.

LONGOVILE
For what?

DUCHESS
This Gentleman, the Lord of Lorne, my Husband,
Will be gone down to shew his play-fellows
Where he is gay.

BEWFORD
What, down into the Countrey?

DUCHESS
Yes faith, was ever fool but he so cross?
I would as fain be gracious to him,
As he could wish me, but he will not let me;
Speak faithfully, will he deserve my mercy?

LONGOVILE
According to his merits he should wear,
A guarded coat, and a great wooden dagger.

DUCHESS
If there be any woman that doth know,
The duties 'twixt a Husband and his wife,
Will speak but one word for him, he shall scape;
Is not that reasonable? but there's none,
Be ready therefore, to pursue the plot
We had against a pinch, for he must stay.

LONGOVILE
Wait you here for him, whilst I goe
And make the King acquainted with your sport,
For fear he be incens'd for our attempting
Places of so great honor.

[Exit **LONGOVILE**.

DUCHESS
Go, be speedy.

[Enter **DUKE**, **COSIN**, **WIFE**, **JAQUES**, **GROOM**.

DUKE
Come let me see how all things are dispos'd of.

JAQUES
One Cart will serve for all your furniture,
With room enough behind to ease the Footman,
A capcase for your linnen, and your plate,
With a strange lock that opens with Amen,
For my young Lord, because of easie portage,
A quiver of your graces lin'd with Cunney,
Made to be hang'd about the Nurses neck,
Thus, with a Scarfe or Towel.

DUKE
Very good.

JAQUES

Nay, 'tis well, but had you staid another week,
I would have had you furnisht, in such pomp,
As never Duke of Burgundy was furnisht,
You should have had a Sumpter, though 't had cost me
The laying on my self, where now you are fain,
To hire a Rippers mare, and buy new dossers,
But I have got them painted with your Arms,
With a fair darnex Carpet of my own
Laid cross for the more state.

DUKE
Jaques I thank you: your Carpet shall be brusht
And sent you home; what, are you ready wife?

DUCHESS
An hour ago.

DUKE
I cannot chuse but kiss thy royal Lips,
Dear Duchess mine, thou art so good a woman.

BEWFORD
Youl'd say so if you knew all, goodman Duckling.

COSIN
This was the happiest fortune could befal me
Now in his absence will I follow close
Mine own preferment, and I hope e'r long,
To make my mean and humble name so strong,
As my great Cosins, when the world shall know,
I bear too hot a spirit to live low.
The next Spring will I down, my wife and houshold,
I'll have my Ushers, and my four Lacquies,
Six spare Caroches too, but mum, no more,
What I intend to do, I'll keep in store.

DUKE
Mountey, mountey, Jaques, be our Querry.

GROOM
To horse there Gentlemen, and fall in couples.

DUKE
Come honoured Duchess.

[Enter **LONGOVILE**.

LONGOVILE

Stand thou proud man.

DUKE
Thieves, Jaques, raise the people.

LONGOVILE
No, raise no people, 'tis the Kings command,
Which bids thee once more stand, thou haughty man,
Thou art a monster, for thou art ungrateful,
And like a fellow of a rebel nature,
Hast flung from his embraces: and for ·
His honors given thee, hast not return'd
So much as thanks, and to oppose his Will,
Resolv'd to leave the Court, and set the Realm
A fire, in discontent, and open action:
Therefore he bids thee stand, thou proud man,
Whilst with the whisking of my sword about,
I take thy honors off: this first sad whisk
Takes off thy Dukedom, thou art but an Earl.

DUKE
You are mistaken, Longovile.

LONGOVILE
Oh would I were: this second whisk divides
Thy Earldom from thee, thou art yet a Baron.

DUKE
No more whisks if you love me Longovile.

LONGOVILE
Two whisks are past, and two are yet behind,
Yet all must come, but not to linger time.
With these two whisks I end, now mount Marine,
For thou art now no more, so says the King,
And I have done his Highness Will with grief.

DUKE
Degraded from my honors?

LONGOVILE
'Tis too certain.

DUKE
I am no Traitor sure, that I know of;
Speak Jaques, hast thou ever heard me utter word
Tending to Treason, or to bring in the enemy?

JAQUES
Alas Sir, I know nothing,
Why should your Worship bring me in to hang me?
God's my judge Gentlemen I never medled
But with the brushing of his cloaths, or fetching
In water in a morning for his hands.

COSIN
Are these the honors of this place? Anthony
Help me to take her Gown off quickly,
Or I'll so swinge ye for't—

WIFE
Why Husband? Sir?

COSIN
I'll not loose a penny by this town.

LONGOVILE
Why what do you mean, Sir, have her to her lodging,
And there undress her, I will wait upon her.

COSIN
Indeed you shall not, your month is out I take it,
Get you out before me wife:
Cosin farewel, I told you long agoe,
That pride begins with pleasure, ends with woe.

[Exit with **WIFE**.

BEWFORD
Goe thy way sentences, 'twill be thy fortune,
To live and dye a Cuckold, and Churchwarden.

DUCHESS
Oh my poor Husband! what a heavy fortune
Is fallen upon him!

BEWFORD
Methinks 'tis strange,
That heaven fore-warning great men of their falls,
With such plain tokens, they should not avoid 'em:
For the last night betwixt eleven and twelve,
Two great and hideous blazing stars were seen
To fight a long hour by the clock, the one
Drest like a Duke, the other like a King;
Till at the last the crowned Star o'er-came.

SERVANT
Why do ye stand so dead, Monsieur Marine?

DUKE
So Cæsar fell, when in the Capitol
They gave his body two and thirty wounds.
Be warned all ye Peers, and by my fall,
Hereafter learn to let your wives rule all.

SERVANT
Monsieur Marine, pray let me speak with you;
Sir, I must wave you to conceal this party,
It stands upon my utter overthrow;
Seem not discontented, nor do not stir afoot,
For if you do, you and your hope—
I swear you are a lost man if you stir.
And have an eye to Bewford, he'll tempt you.

BEWFORD
Come, come, for shame go down;
Were I Marine, by heaven I would go down:
And being there, I would rattle him such an answer
Should make him smoke.

DUKE
Good Monsieur Bewford, peace
Leave these rebellious words,
Or by the honors which I once enjoyed,
And yet may swear by,
I'll tell the King of your proceedings;
I am satisfied.

WIFE
You talkt of going down when 'twas not fit,
But now let's see your spirit,
A thousand and a thousand will expect it.

DUKE
Why wife, are ye mad?

WIFE
No, nor drunk, but I'd have you know your own strength.

DUKE
You talke like a most foolish woman, wife;
I tell you I will stay, yet I have a
Crotchet troubles me.

LONGOVILE
More crotchets yet?

DUKE
Follow me Jaques, I must have thy counsel,
I will return again, stay you there wife.

LONGOVILE
I fear this loss of honor will give him some few stools.

WIFE
No, no, he is resolv'd, he will not
Stir a foot, I'll lay my life.

BEWFORD
I, but he's discontented, how shall we resolve that,
And make him stay with comfort?

WIFE
Faith Bewford we must even let nature work,
For he's the sweetest temper'd man for that
As one can wish, for let men but go about to fool him,
And he'll have his finger as deep in't as the best;
But see where he comes frowning, bless us all!

[Enter **DUKE**.

DUKE
Off with your hats, for here doth come
The high and mighty Duke of Burgundy.
What ever you may think, I have thought
And thought, and thought upon't, and I find it plain,
The King cannot take back what he has given,
Unless I forfeit it by course of Law.
Not all the water in the River Seine,
Can wash the blood out of these Princely veins.

WIFE
God-a-mercy Husband, thou art the best
To work out a thing at a pinch in France.

DUKE
I will ascend my State again,
Duchess, take your place,
And let our Champion enter.

LONGOVILE
Has he his Champion? that's excellent.

DUKE
And let loud Musick sound before his entrance.

[Sound Trumpet.

[Enter **JAQUES** in Armor, carrying a Scutcheon before him, and a two-handed Sword.

WIFE
How well our Champion doth demean himself,
As if he had been made for such an action?
Methinks his sturdy truncheon he doth weild,
Like Mars approaching to a bloody field.

DUKE
I think there's no man so desperate
To dare encounter with our Champion,
But trust me, Jaques, thou hast pleas'd us well;
Once more our warlike Musick, then proceed.

[Enter **SHATTILLION.**

SHATTILLION
What wondrous age is this! what close proceedings!
I hear the clang of Trumpets in this house,
To what intent do not our States-men search?
Oh no, they look not into simple truth;
For I am true, and they regard not me,
A man in Armor too: God save the King,
The world will end, there's nought but treachery.

JAQUES
I Jaques, servant to the high and mighty Godfrey, Duke of Burgundy, do come hither to prove by natural strength, and activity of my body, without the help of sorcery, inchantment, or negromancy, that the said Godfrey, late of Mount Marine, and now of Burgundy, hath perfect right thereto, notwithstanding the Kings command to the contrary, and no other person whatsoever: and in token that I will be ready to make good the same: I throw down my gage, which is my honor, pronounced the 37 of Feb. Stilo novo, God save the Duke.

SHATTILLION
Of all the plots the King hath laid for me
This was the shrewdest, 'tis my life they seek
And they shall have it: if I should refuse
To accept the challenge in the Kings behalf,
They have some cause to take away my life,
And if I do accept it, who can tell,
But I may fall by doubtful chance of War?
'Twas shrew'd, but I must take the least of evils,

I take thy gauntlet up, thou treacherous man,
That stands in armed Coat against the King.
Whom God preserve, and with my single sword,
Will justifie whatever he commands;
I'll watch him for catching of my words.

DUKE
Jaques go on, defend our Princely Title.

SHATTILLION
Why shrink'st thou back? thou hast an evil cause;
Come forward man, I have a rock about me,
I fight for my true Liege.

DUKE
Go forward Jaques.

JAQUES
I do beseech your Grace to pardon me,
I will not fight with him, with any else
I'll shew my resolution speedily.

SHATTILLION
Come, do thy worst, for the King shall see
All is not true, that is reported of me.

JAQUES
I may not fight with him by Law of Arms.

DUKE
What? shall my Title fall? wilt thou not fight?

JAQUES
Never with him that once hath sav'd my life.

SHATTILLION
Dar'st thou not fight? behold then, I do go
Strong with the zeal I bear my Sovereign,
And seize upon that haughty man himself.
Descend the steps (that thou hast thus usurp'd
Against the King and State,) down to the ground,
And if thou do utter but a syllable
To cross the Kings intent, thou art but dead;
There, lye upon the earth, and pine, and dye.
Did ever any man wade through such storms
To save his life, as poor Shattillion?

LONGOVILE

I fear this challenge hath spoil'd all.

Duc. Ne'er fear it, he'll work it out again, servant.
See where Shattillion's Love, poor Lady, comes.

[Enter **LOVE**.

DUKE
Jaques.

JAQUES
Lie still, Sir, if you love your life, I'll whistle when he's gone,

LOVE
Oh Gentlemen, I charge you by the Love
Which you bear to women, take some pitty
On this distressed man, help to restore
That precious Jewel to him he hath lost.

BEWFORD
Lady, what ever power doth lie in us
By Art, or Prayer, or danger, we are yours.

LOVE
A strange conceit hath wrought this malady,
Conceits again must bring him to himself,
My strict denial to his Will wrought this:
And if you could but draw his wilder thoughts
To know me, he would sure recover sense.

LONGOVILE
That charge I'll undertake.

DUKE
Look Jaques, look, for Gods sake let me rise,
This greatness is a jade, I cannot sit it.

JAQUES
His sword is up, and yet he watcheth you.

DUKE
I'll down again, pray for thy Master, Jaques.

SHATTILLION
Now the King may see all the suggestions are not true,
He hath receiv'd against my loyalty;
When all men else refuse, I fight his battels,
And thrust my body into dangers mouth;

I am become his Champion, and this sword
Has taught his enemies to know themselves;
Oh that he would no more be jealous of me!

LONGOVILE
Monsieur Shattillion, the King assigns you,
That for this valiant loyal act of yours,
He hath forgot all jealousies and fears,
And never more will tempt you into danger.

SHATTILLION
But how shall I believe this, what new token
Of reconcilement will he shew me?
Let him release my poor Love from her torment,
From her hard fare, and strict imprisonment.

LONGOVILE
He hath done this to win your after-love,
And see your Lady sent you from the King
By these two Gentlemen: be thankful for her.

SHATTILLION
She lives, she lives, I know her by the power
Shoots from her eyes.

LOVE
Rise dear Shattillion.

SHATTILLION
I know my duty,
Next unto my King, I am to kneel to you.

LOVE
I'll have you rise, fetch me a chair, sit down Shat.

SHATTILLION
I am commanded, and faith tell me Mistriss,
What usage have you had? pray be plain!

LOVE
Oh my most lov'd Shattillion, pain enough,
But now I am free, thanks to my God and King.

LONGOVILE
His eyes grow very heavy, not a word,
That his weak senses may come sweetly home.

SHATTILLION

The King is honourable.

DUKE
When do you whistle Jaques?

JAQUES
By and by.

LONGOVILE
Come hither Monsieur, canst thou laugh a little?

SERVANT
Yes Sir.

LONGOVILE
So thou shalt then. Bewford, how dost thou?

BEWFORD
Why well.

LONGOVILE
I'm glad on't, and how does thy wife?

BEWFORD
Why, you may see her, Sir, she stands behind you.

LONGOVILE
By the mass she's there indeed, but where's her belly?

BEWFORD
Belly?

LONGOVILE
Her great belly, man; what hast thou sent thee?

SERVANT
A Boy, I'll lay my life, it tumbled so.

BEWFORD
Catcht by this light.

LONGOVILE
I'll be a Gossip Bewford.

SERVANT
And I.

LONGOVILE

I have an odd Apostle spoon.

BEWFORD
S'foot, catcht.

DUCHESS
Why, what's the matter, Gentlemen?

LONGOVILE
He's married to your woman.

DUCHESS
And I not know it?

SERVANT
'Twas a venial sin.

BEWFORD
Gall, gall, gall.

DUCHESS
Forgive her, Monsieur Bewford, 'twas her love.

BEWFORD
You may rise if you please, I must endure it.

LONGOVILE
See how my great Lord lies upon the ground
And dare not stir yet!
Jaques whistles?

DUKE
Jaques, Jaques, is the Kings Champion gon yet?

JAQUES
No, but he's asleep.

DUKE
Is he asleep art sure?

JAQUES
I am sure he is, I hear him snore.

DUKE
Then by your favours Gentlemen I rise,
And know I am a Duke still.

JAQUES

And I am his Champion.

DUCHESS
Hold thee there, and all France cannot mend thee.

DUKE
I am a Prince as great within my thoughts
As when the whole state did adorn my person;
What trial can be made to try a Prince?
I will oppose this noble corps of mine
To any danger that may end the doubt.

DUCHESS
Great Duke, and Husband, there is but one way
To satisfie the world of our true right,
And it is dangerous.

DUKE
What may it be?
Were it to bring the great Turk bound in chains
Through France in triumph: or to couple up
The Sophie, and great Prestor John together,
I would attempt it Duchess, tell the course.

DUCHESS
There is a strong opinion through the world,
And no doubt, grounded on experience,
That Lions will not touch a lawful Prince,
If you be confident then of your right,
Amongst the Lions bear your naked body,
And if you come off clear, and never winch,
The world will say you are a perfect Prince.

DUKE
I thank you Duchess, for your kind advice,
But now we do not affect those ravenous beasts.

LONGOVILE
A Lion is a beast to try a King;
But for the trial of such a state like this
Pliny reports a mastive dog will serve.

DUKE
We will not deal with dogs at all, but men.

SERVANT
You shall not need to deal with them at all,
Hark you Sir, the King doth know you are a Duke:

DUKE
No, does he?

SERVANT
Yes, and is content you shall be, but with this caution,
That none know it but your self:
For if ye do, he'll take it away by Act of Parliament.

DUKE
Here's my hand, and whilst I live or breath,
No living wight shall know I am a Duke.

SERVANT
Mark me directly, Sir, your wife may know it.

DUKE
May not Jaques.

SERVANT
Yes, he may.

DUKE
May not my Countrey Cosin?

SERVANT
By no means, Sir, if you love your life and state.

DUKE
Well then, know all, I am no Duke.

SERVANT
No, I'll swear it.

LONGOVILE
See, he wakes.

SHATTILLION
Where am I, or where have I been all this while?
Sleep hath not sate so sound upon mine eyes
But I remember well that face;
Oh thou too cruel, leave at length to scorn
Him that but looking on thy beauty, dies,
Either receive me, or put out my eyes.

LOVE
Dearest Shattillion, see upon my knees,
I offer up my love, forget my wrongs.

SHATTILLION
Art thou mine own?

LOVE
By heaven I am.

SHATTILLION
Then all the world is mine.

LOVE
I have stranger things to tell thee, my dearest love.

SHATTILLION
Tell nothing, but that thou art mine own:
I do not care to know where I have been,
Or how I have liv'd, or any thing,
But that thou art my own.

BEWFORD
Well wife, though 'twere a trick that made us wed,
We'll make our selves merry soon in bed.

DUKE
Know all, I am no Duke.

WIFE
What saye?

DUKE
Jaques?

JAQUES
Sir.

DUKE
I am a Duke.

BOTH
Are ye?

DUKE
Yes faith, yes faith.
But it must only run among our selves,
And Jaques, thou shalt be my Secretary still.

WIFE
Kind Gentlemen, lead in Shattillion,

For he must needs be weak and sickly yet.
Now all my labours have a perfect end, as I could wish,
Let all young sprightly wives that have
Dull foolish coxcombs to their Husbands,
Learn by me their duties, what to do,
Which is, to make 'em fools, and please 'em too.

[Exeunt.

EPILOGUE

The Monuments of virtue, and desert,
Appear more goodly, when the gloss of Art
Is eaten off by time, than when at first
They were set up, not censur'd at the worst.
We'ave done our best, for your contents to fit,
With new pains, this old monument of wit.

Francis Beaumont – A Short Biography

Francis Beaumont was born in 1584 near the small Leicestershire village of Thringstone. Unfortunately precise records of much of his short life do not exist.

He was the son to Sir Francis Beaumont of Grace Dieu, a justice of the common pleas. His mother was Anne, the daughter of Sir George Pierrepont.

The first date we can give for his education is at age 13 when he begins at Broadgates Hall (now Pembroke College, Oxford). Sadly, his father died the following year, 1598. Beaumont left university without a degree and entered the Inner Temple in London in 1600. A career choice of Law taken previously by his father.

The information to hand is confident that Beaumont's career in law was short-lived. He was quickly attracted to the theatre and soon became first an admirer and then a student of poet and playwright Ben Jonson. Jonson at this time was a cultural behemoth; very talented and a life full of volatility that included frequent brushes with the authorities. His followers, including the poet Robert Herrick, were known as 'the sons of Ben'. Beaumont was also on friendly terms with other luminaries such as the poet Michael Drayton.

Beaumont's first work was Salmacis and Hermaphroditus, it debuted in 1602. A 1911 edition of the Encyclopædia Britannica includes the description "not on the whole discreditable to a lad of eighteen, fresh from the popular love-poems of Marlowe and Shakespeare, which it naturally exceeds in long-winded and fantastic diffusion of episodes and conceits."

By 1605, Beaumont had written commendatory verses to Volpone one of Ben Jonson's masterpieces.

It was now, in the early years of the 17th Century, that he met John Fletcher and together they gradually formed one of the most dynamic and productive of writing teams that English theatre has ever produced.

Their playwriting careers at this stage were both troubled by early failure. Beaumont had written The Knight of the Burning Pestle and it was first performed by the Children of the Blackfriars company in 1607. The audience however was distinctly unimpressed. The publisher's epistle in the 1613 quarto says they failed to note "the privie mark of irony about it."

The following year, Fletcher's Faithful Shepherdess failed on the same stage.

In 1609, however, the two collaborated in earnest on Philaster. The play was performed by the King's Men at the Globe Theatre and at Blackfriars. It was a great success. Their careers were now well and truly launched and into the bargain they had ignited and captured a public taste for tragicomedy.

There is an account that at the time the two men shared everything. They lived together in a house on the Bankside in Southwark, " they also lived together in Bankside, sharing clothes and having "one wench in the house between them." Or as another account puts it "sharing everything in the closest intimacy."

This arrangement stopped in about 1613 when Beaumont married Ursula Isley, daughter and co-heiress of Henry Isley of Sundridge in Kent, by whom he had two daughters (one of them was born after his death).

Beaumont, at a very young age even for those times, was struck down by a stroke at some point in mid-1613, after which he was unable to write any more plays, but he did manage to write an elegy for Lady Penelope Clifton, who had died on 26th October 1613.

Francis Beaumont died on March 6th, 1616 and was buried in Westminster Abbey.

In his short life his canon was small but influential. Although he is seen more as a dramatist his poetry was celebrated even then and it continues to gain an avid readership to this day.

It was said at one point of the collaboration of Beaumont and Fletcher that "in their joint plays their talents are so ... completely merged into one, that the hand of Beaumont cannot clearly be distinguished from that of Fletcher." Whilst it was the view then it has not endured into modern times. Indeed, slowly but with certainty the name of Beaumont has been removed from many of their joint works. It has given way to other such luminaries as Philip Massinger, Nathan field and James Shirley.

John Fletcher – A Short Biography

John Fletcher was born in December, 1579 in Rye, Sussex. He was baptised on December 20th.

As can be imagined details of much of his life and career have not survived and, accordingly, only a very brief indication of his life and works can be given.

His father, Richard Fletcher, was a successful and rather ambitious cleric. From being the Dean of Peterborough he moved on to become the Bishop of Bristol, Bishop of Worcester and finally, shortly before his death, the Bishop of London. He was also the chaplain to Queen Elizabeth.

When he was Dean of Peterborough, Richard Fletcher, witnessed the execution of Mary, Queen of Scots. It was said he "knelt down on the scaffold steps and started to pray out loud and at length, in a prolonged and rhetorical style, as though determined to force his way into the pages of history". He cried out at her death, "So perish all the Queen's enemies!" All very dramatic but the family did have strong links to the Arts.

Young Fletcher appears at the very young age of eleven to have entered Corpus Christi College at Cambridge University in 1591. There are no records that he ever took a degree but there is some small evidence that he was being prepared for a career in the church.

However, what is clear is that this was soon abandoned as he joined the stream of people who would leave University and decamp to the more bohemian life of commercial theatre in London.

Unfortunately, his father fell out with Queen Elizabeth but appears to have been on his way to rehabilitation before his death in 1596. At his death he was, however, mired in debt.

The upbringing of the now teenage Fletcher and his seven siblings now passed to his paternal uncle, the poet and minor official Giles Fletcher. Giles, who had the patronage of the Earl of Essex may have been a liability rather than an advantage to the young Fletcher. With Essex involved in the failed rebellion against Elizabeth Giles was also tainted by association.

By 1606 John Fletcher appears to have equipped himself with the talents to become a playwright. Initially this appears to have been for the Children of the Queen's Revels, then performing at the Blackfriars Theatre.

Commendatory verses by Richard Brome in the Beaumont and Fletcher 1647 folio place Fletcher in the company of Ben Jonson, although it is not known when this friendship began. Jonson, of course, was a leviathan of English Literature, so admired that many of his literary friends and colleagues were simply known as 'Sons of Ben'. Fletcher's frequent early collaborator, Francis Beaumont, was also a friend of Jonson's.

Fletcher's early career was marked by one significant failure; The Faithful Shepherdess, his adaptation of Giovanni Battista Guarini's Il Pastor Fido, which was performed by the Blackfriars Children in 1608. In the preface to the printed edition of his play, Fletcher explained the failure as due to his audience's faulty expectations. They expected a pastoral tragicomedy to feature dances, comedy, and murder, with the shepherds presented in conventional stereotypes – as Fletcher put it, wearing "gray cloaks, with curtailed dogs in strings." Fletcher's preface is however best known for its pithy definition of tragicomedy: "A tragicomedy is not so called in respect of mirth and killing, but in respect it wants [i.e., lacks] deaths, which is enough to make it no tragedy; yet brings some near it, which is enough to make it no comedy." A comedy, he went on to say, must be "a representation of familiar people." His preface is critical of drama that features characters whose action violates nature.

In that case, Fletcher appears to have been developing a new style faster than audiences could comprehend. By 1609, however, he had found his stride. With Beaumont, he wrote Philaster, which became a hit for the King's Men and began a profitable association between Fletcher and that company. Philaster appears also to have begun a trend for tragicomedy. Fletcher's influence has also been said to have inspired some features of Shakespeare's late romances, and certainly his influence on the tragicomic work of other playwrights is even more marked.

By the middle of the 1610s, Fletcher's plays had achieved a popularity that rivalled Shakespeare's and cemented the pre-eminence of the King's Men in Jacobean London. After Beaumont's retirement, necessitated by ill-health, and then his early death in 1616, Fletcher continued working, both singly and in collaboration, until his death in 1625. By that time, he had produced, or had been credited with, close to fifty plays. This body of work remained a major part of the King's Men's repertory until the closing of the theatres in 1642 due to the Civil War.

At the beginning of his career Fletcher's most important collaborator was Francis Beaumont. The two wrote together for close to a decade, first for the Children of the Queen's Revels, and then for the King's Men. According to an anecdote transmitted or invented by John Aubrey, they also lived together in Bankside, sharing clothes and having "one wench in the house between them." This domestic arrangement, if it existed, was ended by Beaumont's marriage in 1613, and their dramatic partnership ended after Beaumont fell ill, probably of a stroke, that same year.

At this point Fletcher had written many plays with Beaumont and several others on his own. He seems to have been regarded as quite a talent although it should be remembered that playwrights were required to be prolific, to easily work with other collaborators and to produce work of quality and commercial appeal very quickly.

The King's Men, run by Philip Henslowe, was the most prestigious of the theatre companies and Fletcher now had an increasingly close association with it.

Fletcher collaborated with Shakespeare on Henry VIII, The Two Noble Kinsmen, and the now lost Cardenio, which some scholars say was the basis for Lewis Theobald's play Double Falsehood. (Theobald is regarded as one of the best Shakespearean editors. Whether his play is based on Cardenio or on some other is not absolutely known although Theobald certainly promoted it as his revision of the lost Shakespeare/Fletcher play.)

A play that Fletcher also wrote by himself at this time, The Woman's Prize or the Tamer Tamed, is also regarded as a sequel to The Taming of the Shrew.

In 1616, with the death of Shakespeare, Fletcher now appears to have entered into an enhanced arrangement with the King's Men on very similar terms to Shakespeare's. Fletcher would now write exclusively for the King's Men until his own death almost a decade later.

As well as continuing his solo productions Fletcher was still collaborating with other playwrights, mainly Philip Massinger, who, in turn, would succeed him as the in-house playwright for the King's Men.

Fletcher's popularity continued throughout his life; indeed, during the winter of 1621, he had three of his plays performed at court. His mastery is most notable in two dramatic types; tragicomedy and the comedy of manners.

John Fletcher died in 1625, it is thought of bubonic plague which, at the time, was undergoing further outbreaks.

He seems to have been buried in what is now Southwark Cathedral, although a precise location is not known. There is much made of an anecdote that Fletcher and Massinger (who died in 1640) share the same grave but it is more likely that both are buried within a few yards of each other and that the stone markers in the floor have confused the issue. One is marked 'Edmond Shakespeare 1607' and the other 'John Fletcher 1625' refers to Shakespeare's younger brother and the playwright. The churchyards were, more often than not, completely over-crowded and breeding grounds for disease. Precise record keeping was not a practiced skill.

During the later Commonwealth, many of the playwright's best-known scenes were kept alive as drolls. These were brief performances, usually condensed into one or two scenes and with the addition of music or song to satisfy the taste for plays while the theatres were closed under the Puritans. At the re-opening of the theatres in 1660, the plays in the Fletcher canon, in original form or revised, were by far the most common productions on the English stage. The most frequently revived plays suggest the developing taste for comedies of manners. Among the tragedies, The Maid's Tragedy and, especially, Rollo Duke of Normandy held the stage. Four tragicomedies (A King and No King, The Humorous Lieutenant, Philaster, and The Island Princess) were popular, perhaps in part for their similarity to and foreshadowing of heroic drama. Four comedies (Rule a Wife And Have a Wife, The Chances, Beggars' Bush, and especially The Scornful Lady) were also stage mainstays.

Despite his popularity, and it appears he was held in higher regard than Shakespeare at this time, his works steadily lost ground to those of Shakespeare and to new productions from other playwrights.

Since then Fletcher has increasingly become a subject only for occasional revivals and for specialists. Fletcher and his collaborators have been the subject of important bibliographic and critical studies, but the plays have been revived only infrequently.

Due to the frequent collaborations between all manner of playwrights, and the revisions carried out in later years, having a settled list of authorship to any given set of plays can be problematic. The works of Fletcher and others of this period most definitely fall into this category. It is as well to take into account that during this period theatres were quite often closed either due to outbreaks of the plague or to the prevailing political and moral climate. Printers, anxious to provide materials that would sell, were not above changing a name or two to enhance sales.

Although Fletcher collaborated most often with Beaumont and Massinger, it is believed that Massinger revised many of the plays some time after their original production. Other collaborators including Nathan Field, William Shakespeare, William Rowley and others also can be seen distinctly in Fletchers' works. Many modern scholars point out that Fletcher had many particular mannerisms, but other playwrights would also duplicate these at times so allocating exact contributions of anyone to a play is somewhat of a detective case in many instances. However, from the original folio printings or licensing via the Master of the Revels (the statutory licensing authority to approve and censor plays as well a hand in publication and printing of theatrical materials) as well as contemporary notes a fairly precise bibliography of the works can be given with only a few plays lacking substantial authority and provenance.

Francis Beaumont & John Fletcher – A Concise Bibliography

This bibliography gives the most likely date of writing together with when published, revised or licensed by the Master or the Revels (This position within the royal household was originally for royal festivities, ie revels, and later to oversee stage censorship, until this function was transferred to the Lord Chamberlain in 1624).

Francis Beaumont – Solo Plays
The Knight of the Burning Pestle, comedy (performed 1607; printed 1613)
The Masque of the Inner Temple and Gray's Inn, masque (printed 1613)

John Fletcher - Solo Plays
The Faithful Shepherdess, pastoral (written 1608–9; printed 1609)
The Tragedy of Valentinian, tragedy (1610–14; 1647)
Monsieur Thomas, comedy (c. 1610–16; 1639)
The Woman's Prize, or The Tamer Tamed, comedy (c. 1611; 1647)
Bonduca, tragedy (1611–14; 1647)
The Chances, comedy (c. 1613–25; 1647)
Wit Without Money, comedy (c. 1614; 1639)
The Mad Lover, tragicomedy (acted 5 January 1617; 1647)
The Loyal Subject, tragicomedy (licensed 16 November 1618; revised 1633; 1647)
The Humorous Lieutenant, tragicomedy (c. 1619; 1647)
Women Pleased, tragicomedy (c. 1619–23; 1647)
The Island Princess, tragicomedy (c. 1620; 1647)
The Wild Goose Chase, comedy (c. 1621; 1652)
The Pilgrim, comedy (c. 1621; 1647)
A Wife for a Month, tragicomedy (licensed 27 May 1624; 1647)
Rule a Wife and Have a Wife, comedy (licensed 19 October 1624; 1640)

Francis Beaumont & John Fletcher
The Woman Hater, comedy (1606; 1607)
Cupid's Revenge, tragedy (c. 1607–12; 1615)
Philaster, or Love Lies a-Bleeding, tragicomedy (c. 1609; 1620)
The Maid's Tragedy, Tragedy (c. 1609; 1619)
A King and No King, tragicomedy (1611; 1619)
The Captain, comedy (c. 1609–12; 1647)
The Scornful Lady, comedy (c. 1613; 1616)
Love's Pilgrimage, tragicomedy (c. 1615–16; 1647)
The Noble Gentleman, comedy (c. 1613; licensed 3 February 1626; 1647)

Their Collaborations with Others

With Philip Massinger
Thierry & Theodoret, tragedy (c. 1607; 1621)
The Coxcomb, comedy (c. 1608–10; 1647)
Beggars' Bush, comedy (c. 1612–13; revised 1622; 1647)

Love's Cure, comedy (c. 1612–13; revised 1625; 1647)

John Fletcher with Philip Massinger
Sir John van Olden Barnavelt, tragedy (August 1619; MS)
The Little French Lawyer, comedy (c. 1619–23; 1647)
A Very Woman, tragicomedy (c. 1619–22; licensed 6 June 1634; 1655)
The Custom of the Country, comedy (c. 1619–23; 1647)
The Double Marriage, tragedy (c. 1619–23; 1647)
The False One, history (c. 1619–23; 1647)
The Prophetess, tragicomedy (licensed 14 May 1622; 1647)
The Sea Voyage, comedy (licensed 22 June 1622; 1647)
The Spanish Curate, comedy (licensed 24 October 1622; 1647)
The Lovers' Progress or The Wandering Lovers, tragicomedy (licensed 6 December 1623; rev 1634; 1647)
The Elder Brother, comedy (c. 1625; 1637)

John Fletcher with Philip Massinger & Nathan Field
The Honest Man's Fortune, tragicomedy (1613; 1647)
The Queen of Corinth, tragicomedy (c. 1616–18; 1647)
The Knight of Malta, tragicomedy (c. 1619; 1647)

John Fletcher with William Shakespeare
Henry VIII, history (c. 1613; 1623)
The Two Noble Kinsmen, tragicomedy (c. 1613; 1634)
Cardenio, tragicomedy (c. 1613)

John Fletcher with Thomas Middleton & William Rowley
Wit at Several Weapons, comedy (c. 1610–20; 1647)

John Fletcher with William Rowley
The Maid in the Mill (licensed 29 August 1623; 1647).

John Fletcher with Nathan Field
Four Plays, or Moral Representations, in One, morality (c. 1608–13; 1647)

John Fletcher with Philip Massinger, Ben Jonson and George Chapman
Rollo Duke of Normandy, or The Bloody Brother, tragedy (c. 1617; revised 1627–30; 1639)

John Fletcher with James Shirley
The Night Walker, or The Little Thief, comedy (c. 1611; 1640)
The Coronation c. 1635

Uncertain
The Nice Valour, or The Passionate Madman, comedy (c. 1615–25; 1647)
The Laws of Candy, tragicomedy (c. 1619–23; 1647)
The Fair Maid of the Inn, comedy (licensed 22 January 1626; 1647)
The Faithful Friends, tragicomedy (registered 29 June 1660; MS.)

The Nice Valour is possibly by Fletcher revised by Thomas Middleton;

The Fair Maid of the Inn is perhaps a play by Massinger, John Ford, and John Webster, either with or without Fletcher's involvement.

The Laws of Candy has been variously attributed to Fletcher and to John Ford.

The Night-Walker was a Fletcher original, with additions by Shirley for a 1639 production.

Even now there is not absolute certainty on several of the plays. The first Beaumont & Fletcher folio of 1647 contained 35 plays and the second folio of 1679 added a further 18. In total 53 plays.

The first folio included The Masque of the Inner Temple and Gray's Inn (1613), and the second The Knight of the Burning Pestle (1607), widely considered Beaumont's solo works, although the latter was in early editions attributed to both writers. Fletcher himself said that Beaumont was attributed co-authorship of many works that belonged solely to Fletcher or to other collaborators.

One play in the canon, Sir John Van Olden Barnavelt, existed in manuscript and was not published till 1883.

www.ingramcontent.com/pod-product-compliance
Lightning Source LLC
Chambersburg PA
CBHW060121050426

42448CB00010B/1982